GENESIS

THE UNTOLD STORY

GENESIS

THE UNTOLD STORY

A Refreshing Look at Our Owner's Manual

By Lisa Aiken & Ira Michaels

First Edition MMVII

Copyright © MMVII by Lisa Aiken and Ira Michaels

Cover by Hash Marks Productions
Supervising Artist: Hillel Smith

Editing and Layout by Rossi Pub.
Supervising Editor: Rebecca Lane

Production Manager: Adam Simon

ISBN 0-9779629-1-1

For information regarding bulk purchases and non-profit discounts
please contact the publisher.

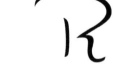

ROSSI PUBLICATIONS
269 South Beverly Drive Suite 296
Beverly Hills, CA 90212
310-867-6328

www.RossiPublications.com

10 9 8 7 6 5 4 3 2 1

This book is dedicated to the memory of

Mordechai Yoel ben Yitzchak Dovid, *a'h*
May it bring merit to his soul.

It is the authors' wish that this book sanctify God's Name and inspire all who read it to come closer to our Creator. May our children and their descendants forever love studying Torah and joyfully live in accordance with its ways.

Approbation

from Rabbi Avigdor Neventzahl SHLI'TA,
Chief Rabbi of The Old City of Jerusalem and
Senior Rosh Yeshiva of Yeshivat Netiv Aryeh

I greatly enjoyed seeing a book that deals with this topic, bringing the reader closer to the Tanach (Bible), specifically the teachings of our Sages of blessed memory and the many great personalities throughout the generations. The authors should have success in all their holy endeavors and bring all of the Jewish People closer to their Father in heaven. They should be blessed with a good year, be signed and sealed for good, and soon see the coming of the Messiah, our redeemer, who will help us all to have a wholehearted return to our Father in heaven. The authors should only see good things in all of their days.

Avigdor Neventzahl

CONTENTS

Acknowledgments

We would like to thank many people who made this book possible, especially our many teachers whose ideas influenced and informed our writing of this book.

The brilliant insights of Mrs. Tzippora Heller; Rabbi Yitzchok Kirzner, z"tl; and Rabbi Uziel Milevsky, z"tl, changed our understanding of Torah and Midrash.

Sara Malka Laderman's amazing editing turned a rough stone into a diamond. Adam Simon's meticulous attention and backing was outstanding. Hillel Smith's patience and artistry are so appreciated. And last, but not least, the editing and production staff at Rossi Publications are a pleasure to work with.

We thank all of you from the bottom of our hearts.

This book was 14 years in the making. We are grateful to the Almighty that it finally has come to fruition.

Lisa Aiken and Ira Michaels
Jerusalem, 5768

Foreword

Searching for spirituality?

Like many Jews, the last place you'd probably look is Genesis. Creation, Adam and Eve, The Garden of Eden, Noah and the Flood— these stories may seem uneducated and childish. It's hard to sift fact from fraud in more than 2,000 years of efforts by the Greeks through 21st-century scientists to discredit the Bible. And muddying the waters of truth are "great" religions that rely on mistranslated Biblical passages to bolster their doctrines.

It's a jungle out there. Yet our hearts sense that somewhere in the world is a source of truth and timeless wisdom that seems to lie just beyond our grasp.

If we were to write a Bible today, how would we want it to speak to us? We would want it to tell us about God and how we can connect to Him. It would appeal to our rational, mystical, and emotional selves. We would expect it to explain why there is evil and suffering in the world. This Bible would inform us how to get the most out of life and what that life's purpose is. And of course it would help us find comfort and direction in our times of challenge and disappointment.

We already have this very Bible: The Five Books of Moses.[1] Known to Jews as the Torah ("teaching"), it has done for the Jewish people for 3,300 years what we modern people want a Bible to do today. However, some of us may have misplaced the tools that help us access this great wisdom. The first step in regaining our tools may be to learn how we lost them in the first place.

* * *

In the 18th century, the Enlightenment movement swept across Europe. Its premise was that people didn't need religion. Scientific understanding and human logic would lead to true knowledge, peace, and social progress. For the Jews specifically, getting civil rights and secular education and assimilating into the surrounding Gentile culture became sought-after goals.[2] In the late 18th and early 19th centuries, Napoleon granted political equality to the Jews in the aftermath of the French Revolution. Jews were allowed to have basic rights previously denied them as long as they agreed to renounce foreign allegiance and vow allegiance to the French empire. Many French Jews raced to abandon their ties to the Land of Israel and Jewish nationalism to become French citizens. Across Western Europe, Jews who believed that traditional Judaism was outmoded and an obstacle to their social and economic advancement left the faith. More than 250,000 Jews in Central Europe alone converted to Christianity in the 19th century.[3]

Although Napoleon was defeated in Russia, he brought the ideas of the French Revolution—the belief that secular education, human reason, and the abandonment of religion would bring a better world—to Poland and Russia.[4] Eastern European Jews in the 19th century wanted to escape from unrelenting poverty and frequent pogroms. Some believed that they could escape anti-Semitism and gain acceptance by the Czar by subscribing to a "Jewish culture" that was devoid of Jewish religious observances and beliefs. These secular Jews largely gave up their connection with their traditional knowledge and way of life, stopped studying the Torah, and stopped passing on the Torah's traditions and wisdom to successive generations.[5]

In 19th-century Germany, Abraham Geiger invented Reform Judaism in an attempt to adapt the ancient Jewish faith to an "enlightened" world. He believed that Jews should completely reject all institutions of traditional Judaism as well as Talmudic Judaism.[6] The first Reform temple opened in Germany in 1810 and innovated German songs, sermons, prayers, a choir with men and women, and a host of other changes in the traditional Jewish prayer services and setting. German Jews largely turned their backs on the noisy and "unenlightened" traditional synagogue in favor of these new Reform temples, or they flocked to the orderly Lutheran church.[7]

In 1819, some "intellectual" German Jews founded the *Wissenschaft des Judentum* school. Using secular "scholarship," they sought to deny the Divine authorship of the Bible and create a modern form of Judaism that would gain them acceptance by the non-Jewish world.[8]

In the 1870s, Julius Wellhausen, an anti-Semitic Protestant theologian,[9] began a movement of "Higher Biblical Criticism." His view of the Torah as a man-made concoction spread to universities in Western Europe and America. Its general premises are espoused in popular books and are used to teach university students about the Jewish Bible today.[10] His perspective attacks the divine origins of the Torah and dismisses it by "proving" that the Torah consists of four separate documents written by different authors at different times that were "doctored" by priestly canonizers during the Second Temple era. He claimed that these authors did this to perpetuate the "lie" that Moses authored the Torah and that the Jews had a central place of worship in the Tabernacle and later in the Temple. Wellhausen insisted that there never was a Tabernacle, nor was there a revelation of the Torah at Sinai to the Jewish people, and that Moses, if he existed, believed in a local thunder or mountain god. In summation, Wellhausen delegitimized the Jews' religion, their history, and their traditional ways of understanding the Torah by claiming that the Torah was a complete forgery and not a written account of God's words to Moses and the Jewish people.[11]

Because of these events, most people only have shallow and literal understandings of Torah stories stripped of their deeper meaning. Although these distorted teachings have a strong voice, they have robbed Jews and the world of the great value to be found in the Five Books of Moses.

Just as our knowledge of school subjects becomes more sophisticated as we grow older, so must our understanding of the Bible. The Torah is grasped differently when we are 60 years old than when we are 6. *Genesis: The Untold Story* revisits the stories in Genesis—illuminated by traditional Jewish commentaries, history, science, and psychology—to present a logical and mature view of God and His plan for us.

These stories can then be used just as they were originally intended: to inform our lives as we change and grow wiser. The result is a relevant guide to living in the modern world.

Notes

1. These books are Genesis, Exodus, Leviticus, Numbers, and Deuteronomy. Some people refer to all 24 books of the Jewish canon as the Torah, although they are more accurately called by the acronym *Tanach* (*Torah, Neviim, Ketuvim*)—the Five Books of Moses, the Books of the Prophets, and the Holy Writings. The term *Torah* can also refer to the Five Books of Moses plus their explication by the Oral Law. When this book refers to the Torah, it means the Five Books of Moses unless otherwise indicated.

2. Wein, Berel. *Triumph of Survival*. Shaar Press, Brooklyn, 1990, pp. 43-44.

3. Johnson, Paul. *A History of the Jews*. Harper and Row, New York, 1987, p. 312.

4. Wein, Berel, *Triumph of Survival*, Shaar Press, Brooklyn, 1990, p. 76.

5. *Ibid.*, pp. 152-172 for a detailed description of those times.

6. Johnson, Paul. *A History of the Jews*. Harper and Row, New York, 1987, p. 334.

7. By the mid-19th century, Reform leaders argued that "Berlin is our Jerusalem." Samuel Holdheim, who headed the Reform congregation in Berlin, maintained that Jews should not circumcise their sons, use Hebrew, or mention Zion, Jerusalem, or Israel in their prayers, blow the shofar on the New Year, believe in a Messiah, or wear a head covering or prayer shawl while praying; and he changed the Sabbath day to the Christian Sunday. Reform Jews described themselves as "Germans of the Mosaic persuasion," but not as Jews. See Berel Wein, *Triumph of Survival*, Shaar Press, Brooklyn, 1990, p. 53.

8. The society disintegrated when its members converted to Christianity. Wein, Berel. *Triumph of Survival*, p. 55.

9. Like nearly all Christians of the time, the proponents of "Higher Biblical Criticism" believed in the moral superiority of Christianity to Judaism, and they used their scholarly works to illustrate this. Wellhausen, for example, likened Judaism in late antiquity to a dead tree. He said of the Biblical Book of Chronicles, "Like ivy it overspreads the dead trunk with extraneous life, blending old and new in a strange combination. . . . [I]n the process it is twisted and perverted." Excerpted from Terry Gross, "'How to Read the Bible' Through History," *Fresh Air* from WHYY, NPR radio, January 30, 2006.

10. Wellhausen was not the first to attack belief in the Divine authorship of the Torah, but he succeeded in popularizing his beliefs. Benedictus de Spinoza, an apostate British Jew, did so in the 17th century. Jean Astruc (1684-1766), a French physician, is considered the real founder of classical Bible Criticism. Karl Graf (1815-1869) was a German Protestant Bible scholar on whose work Wellhausen founded his theory. Wellhausen's forerunners were Karl Ilgen (1763-1834), a German Protestant philologist; Wilhelm Leberecht de Wette (1780-1849); and Wilhelm Vatke (1806-1882). Vatke laid the foundation for Wellhausen's critique, and the latter admitted that he was indebted to Vatke "for the most and the best" of his own work.

Ironically, Vatke later retracted his conclusions, undermining many theories that Wellhausen later published! For a brilliant discussion of the origins and progression of Higher Biblical Criticism, see Rabbi Nathan Lopes Cardozo, "Of Silence and Speech," 1995, reprinted on "Bible Criticism and its Counterarguments," simpletoremember.com.

11. In cases where Wellhausen needed to change the plain meaning of a Hebrew word to fit into this theory, he offered "conjectural emendation." The fact that thousands of verses contradicted his theory never disturbed him. He contended that a master forger or interpolator had anticipated Wellhausen's theory and consequently inserted passages and changed verses in bits and pieces, as was necessary, so as to refute it. Rabbi Nathan Lopes Cardozo, "Of Silence and Speech," 1995, reprinted on "Bible Criticism and its Counterarguments," simpletoremember.com.

Preface: The Jewish Toolbox

Here are some of the tools we will use to gain a fuller appreciation of the Torah stories:

Reconnecting to the Oral Law

Our first tool is our national treasure-trove of stories, explanations, and legacies—some dating as far back as Moses—known as our Oral Law, so named because this information was to be kept in its fluid state and not written down. When Christians burned the Talmud in the Middle Ages, it was our connection to our Oral Law that they were trying to destroy. Let's understand how the Oral Law relates to Genesis.

Until a few centuries ago, Jews were so familiar with Judaism that even children understood the written Torah, or Written Law, as the "Cliff Notes" of the Jews' history and of the laws by which they lived. For example, although the Torah tells us to keep the Sabbath, nowhere do the Five Books of Moses mention doing so by lighting Sabbath candles, saying a prayer over wine, or eating loaves of bread known as *challah*. It is the Oral Law that tells us how to follow the cryptic commandment "Remember the Sabbath day to keep it holy." Many other examples, such as definitions for *mezuzah* (words of the Torah written on parchment and placed on doorposts) and *tefillin* (black boxes containing Torah verses written on parchment that Jewish men place on their arms and heads every morning) are given short shrift in the written Torah but are explained at length in the vast Oral Law.

Jews of prior generations also knew and understood the Torah's allusions to traditions about its deepest meanings and how to apply its laws to life events. Many of these traditions and elaborations were given to Moses when he received the written Torah on Mount Sinai. Over time, legal judgments and interpretations by the Jewish nation's top judges and Torah interpreters joined the original oral transmission.

Moses taught both Written and Oral Law to the Israelites during their 40 years in the desert. Jews continued to pass down the written Torah and its growing body of Oral Law via parents and extended family, priests, and teachers from one generation to the next, as noted in *Ethics of the Fathers* (*Pirkei Avot*) and other Jewish sources. Fearing a disruption of the oral transmission due to persecution, the Jews wrote down the Oral Law (in Hebrew) as the *Mishnah* by the year 200. As the Mishnah was adapted to new situations and required elaboration, new material plus older laws and stories (*aggadah*) that were not originally included in the Mishnah were recorded (in Aramaic) as the *Gemarra* by the year 500. The *Talmud* consists of the Mishnah and its explanation and the Gemarra. For the past 1500 years, additional explanations and determinations of how to apply Talmudic law to daily life have been added by famous and learned Jewish scholars.

Today, some 80 generations later, our Oral Law still informs us of how we can best understand ourselves and how our Creator wants us to live.

Understanding PaRDeS

The second set of tools is called PaRDeS, the initials of the four main ways of understanding the Torah. They are as follows:

(a) literal meaning of the text (*peshat*);
(b) veiled textual hints that convey important ideas (*remez*);
(c) symbolic stories that teach us (*derash*); and
(d) mystical concepts (*sod*).

These four levels of commentary are often printed alongside traditional Hebrew versions of the Bible as well as in other, well-known books by outstanding and learned Torah commentators. Whenever we encounter poorly written verses, such as redundancies, inconsistencies, or ideas that don't make sense, we can use these red flags to key us into additional lessons to be learned via one or more of these four methods of interpretation. Ultimately, all of these lessons have some moral or spiritual relevance to our lives. We will draw on this treasury throughout this book.

Returning to Hebrew

Reading the Torah in the original ancient Hebrew is far superior to reading a translation. In translation, syntax, grammar, and accuracy may be lost, and many layers of meaning underlying the choice of words and even the shapes of letters will elude us. If reading Shakespeare in Chinese just isn't Shakespeare, how much more is this true of a book with a Divine Author!

Genesis: The Untold Story translates many Biblical verses literally to show why some verses invite or require elaboration or interpretation—and what we can learn from them. We include insights from several traditional Bible commentaries, Rashi (an acronym for Rabbeinu Shlomo Yitchaki) being the most prominent. This brilliant medieval French rabbi (and vintner) elucidated the Biblical text's literal meaning as well as referenced appropriate metaphorical stories (*midrash*) to explain hidden ideas in the verses.

Dispelling Distortion

Unfortunately, much of what we think we know today of the Hebrew Bible is based on mistranslations from the original Hebrew,[1] misinformation, and deliberate distortions of the Torah's ideas by other religions. For example, secularists lacking extensive traditional Torah knowledge take the Bible's many anthropomorphisms (describing God as having human attributes) literally and insist that the early Jews thought that God had human emotions. Yet traditional Jews at an early age are taught that God wrote the Torah in human terms to accommodate limits in human understanding, and that apparent anthropomorphisms exist throughout the Torah to help us relate to divine actions. This is but one example of how the Torah is distorted by those who don't appreciate—or aren't informed of—traditional commentary.

Deliberate distortion also occurred by other religions to justify their new tenets. For example, although Christians accept the Old Testament as holy and believe that God publicly revealed the Five

3

Books of Moses to the entire Jewish people, they mistranslated part of Isaiah so it would appear to predict a Virgin Birth. (The Hebrew verse in Isaiah 7:14 mentions a "young woman"; the Christian version turns her into a "virgin").

Moslems accept Moses as a prophet; Mohammed based many of the Koran's teachings on stories and laws from the Torah (which preceded the Koran by some 2,000 years). He also incorporated some basic rituals and ideas, such as belief in one God, prayer, reciting a verse proclaiming God's unity, and giving to charity, that he borrowed from our Torah and/or Talmud without noting that they have their source in Judaism. Thus, some Moslems teach that Abraham brought his son Isaac as an offering in Mecca, or that he brought Ishmael as an offering on Mount Moriah, instead of teaching that he brought Isaac on Mount Moriah, as the Torah teaches. While the Torah says that Jacob lay down and dreamed of angels ascending and descending a ladder to Heaven (Jewish commentaries located that event on Mount Moriah), some Moslems replaced this incident with Mohammed's night journey to Heaven from Mount Moriah in an attempt to legitimize the Moslems' claim to the Temple Mount in Jerusalem.

Understanding Our Raison d'Être

Judaism teaches that the Almighty gave the Jews[2] the Torah so we could optimize our time in this material world. Without the Torah, we would not know how to use our bodies or the world to bring eternal meaning to our lives, or how to conduct the most meaningful relationships with people and our Creator. As our souls' owner's manual, it guides us to work hard to do God's will.

When life in this world is over, our souls go to a spiritual afterlife to enjoy an intimacy with Him that we spent a lifetime earning. The more we have done God's will, the more we will have earned the greatest pleasure possible—an eternal closeness with our Heavenly Parent.[3]

The Torah expresses our Creator's will and "mind," and studying His Guidebook should be a joyous, exciting, and intellectually stimulating treasure hunt. The prizes we get at the end are the awe we feel at its Author's wisdom, the clarity it gives about our lives, and the resulting love we feel for the One Who gave us this tremendous gift.

Please join us on our journey through Genesis, and may its Author grant us a full, clear, and sweet understanding of His Holy Torah.

Notes

1. The Torah was first translated from its original Hebrew about 250 BCE (Before the Common Era), when King Ptolemy of Egypt forced 72 Jewish Sages to independently translate the Five Books of Moses into Greek. The rabbis deliberately mistranslated the same 15 verses (miraculously, each rabbi used the same words) so that the pagan Greeks would not get the wrong ideas from a literal translation of the text (Babylonian Talmud, *Megillah* 9a-b). Because translating the Torah into another language could open it up to misunderstandings and would involve missed opportunities for deeper understanding, this incident was considered a tragedy in Jewish history. The resulting Greek text is known as the Septuagint, meaning "seventy" in Greek, so named after the number of translators.

   Although the Septuagint contained deliberate mistranslations, it was not a distortion, as the intent was to make the traditionally understood meanings clearer. However, the next mistranslation was very different. Jerome translated the Hebrew Scriptures into Latin in the early 5th century CE (Common Era; Christians refer to this time as AD). This translation was called the Vulgate. Besides creating a poor translation due to a lack of Latin equivalents for many Hebrew words, Jerome was a Christian who knew little Hebrew and whose purpose was to prove that Jesus and Christianity were foretold in the Old Testament. He rearranged the order of the Old Testament books such that the Jewish canon then deceptively ended with the Book of Malachi instead of with the Book of Chronicles. Malachi's last verses predict the coming of Elijah the Prophet and the apocalypse. The New Testament immediately follows with the description of Jesus' story, as if to say that Malachi had predicted the Messiah's advent and the prediction had come true with the founder of Christianity.

   Jerome deliberately falsified (and misunderstood) hundreds of verses to further mislead readers into thinking that Jesus and Christianity were foretold in the earlier books of the Jews. For example, he mistranslated Zechariah 12:10-11 to read,

   > I will pour out on the house of David and on the inhabitants of Jerusalem the Spirit of grace and supplication, and they will look onto **Me** whom [*et asher*] they have pierced and they will mourn for **Him** as one mourns for an only son, and they will weep for Him like the weeping over a first born. In that day there will be a great mourning in Jerusalem like the mourning of Hadadrimmon in the plain of Megiddo.

   Jerome conveniently dropped the Hebrew word *et* and capitalized the word *him* to make a point that was not conveyed in the Hebrew. The translated verse should read,

   > . . . the spirit of grace and supplication, and they will look toward Me because of those whom they have stabbed, they will mourn over him as one mourns for an only child. . . .

   Jerome's mistranslation implies that these verses refer to Jesus instead of to the righteous King Josiah, who abolished idolatry in Israel and was killed in battle with Pharaoh Neco (II Kings 23:29-30) at Megiddo. According to the Talmud (*Moed Katan* 28b), these verses actually mean that all of Judah and Jerusalem mourned when Josiah, referred to in this verse as Hadadrimmon, died (II Chronicles 35:22-25). Just as Jews then mourned over King Josiah, who died in battle when he was pierced by a spear, the verse predicted that the Jewish people in the future would mourn over their war dead. These verses also allude to the Jews' mourning for King Ahab, who was killed by Hadadrimmon.

Habbakuk 3:18 says, "Yet I will rejoice in God, I will feel joy in the God of my salvation." Jerome distorted it to read, "I shall rejoice in my God Jesus." Jerome took the Hebrew word *yishee*, meaning "my salvation," and substituted the word *yeshu*, the Hebrew word for Jesus.

In 1611, the King James Version of the Old Testament resulted from translating the Vulgate into English. The American Bible Society in the 19th century examined six editions of the King James Bible then circulating and found 24,000 variants in the text and punctuation!

2. The Torah is unique in being the only Holy Book of a religion that was revealed publicly for all to see. Those of all other religions were revealed to just a few privileged individuals. The Torah was revealed to three million or so Jews 3,319 years ago in a public place, Mount Sinai, for all to witness.

3. Non-Jews can attain closeness to, and eternal spiritual intimacy with, God by following the seven Noahide principles that encompass approximately 70 of the Torah's 613 laws.

Part I:
In the Beginning

Concepts of Creation

In the beginning, God created the heavens and the earth. And the earth was empty and chaotic and darkness [was] on the face of the deep, and the spirit of God blew on the face of the water. And God said, "Let there be light, and there was light. And God saw the light, that it was good, and God divided between the light and the dark. And God called the light "day" and the darkness He called "night." And there was evening and there was morning one day.[1]

Summary: During the next five days, God created a firmament, upper and lower waters, dry land, vegetation, the sun, the moon, the stars, and various forms of animal life, plus people.

Creation vs. Eternal Universe

For millennia, many educated people rejected the Bible because these verses in Genesis seem impossible or anti-scientific. Famous philosophers as far back as Aristotle, and scientists[2] until the 1960s (when the Big Bang theory was substantiated), ridiculed the Torah's account of Creation. They insisted that the universe could not have been created, since it is impossible for something to be created from nothing. They were sure that matter and time existed forever, and that there was no Creator. They believed that the world was always here and would always be here. Since many educated people believe what philosophers and scientists teach about the world, they rejected the Bible's ideas about Creation.

What was behind their reasoning? The majority of Western philosophers and scientists wanted to believe that there was no Creator and no moral purpose to life. However, their assumptions about how the world is put together began to unravel in the 20th century, thus making it reasonable that God created the world. Let's see how this happened:

In 1905, Einstein proposed his theory of relativity to explain how the universe operates. The theory revolutionized the way scientists viewed the world, because it claimed that time was not invariable, but rather is relative to how fast something is moving. This is a difficult concept for us to comprehend because that is not what we experience.

People today take for granted that gravity affects weight. We have all seen movies of astronauts leaping about the surface of the moon like ballet stars with springs on their feet. How can they do this? Because weaker gravity on the moon means that people or objects weigh only one-sixth of their Earthly weight. Although we understand that weight can vary, we assume that time doesn't vary because we don't experience time actually moving slower or faster. But time does vary, as proven by modern experiments.[3]

Einstein's theory of relativity opened the door to question many other fundamental assumptions about the world. For example, was the world really eternal? If not, it was possible that a Creator made the world. Einstein himself believed in a divine force, although he did not accept Biblical explanations of Creation. He opposed them so much that his feelings caused him to skew his scientific theories: He proposed equations assuming that the earth was static, but then had to use "fudge factors" to make his equations work.[4]

In 1916, drafts of Einstein's theory of general relativity were first circulated. When Danish mathematician William de Sitter reviewed it, he wrote Einstein that the theory had problems that could only be solved by proposing that the universe was expanding in all directions from a central point. This implied that the universe was not eternal, but that it had come into being at a certain point in time and was still coming into being. Einstein didn't respond to his letter.

In 1922, Soviet mathematician Alexander Friedmann independently discovered that Einstein's equations only worked if the universe were exploding away from a central point. Meanwhile, in the United States, astronomer Vesto Slipher noted a similar phenomenon: the 42 galaxies that he discovered by 1925, beginning with the Andromeda galaxy in 1913, were all rocketing away from Earth.

When these three men shared their findings with Einstein, Einstein begrudgingly admitted that they were probably right. Yet he didn't like the implications that the universe wasn't static. If it originated from nothing, that implied a Creator. He told a colleague, "I have not yet fallen in the hands of priests."[5] He wrote de Sitter, "This circumstance [of an expanding universe, which implied a Creator and moment of Creation] irritates me."[6] His comments remind us of how even supposedly objective scientists can be blinded to the truth when it has moral or religious implications.

Still, Einstein could reassure himself that 42 receding galaxies did not a universe make. It was still possible that most of the universe was static. But in 1929, using the world's largest telescope, Edwin Hubble showed that every galaxy within 100,000,000 light years of Earth was receding. This was pretty convincing evidence that the universe as a whole was expanding. And if that were true, and Einstein's equations were run backwards, it implied that the universe once had a beginning.

In 1946, George Gamow and his colleagues proposed that an enormous source of energy—a "primeval fireball"—appeared out of nothing and began the universe.[7] This was the source of all the matter that now exists in the universe. Their theory predicted that all of the galaxies in the universe should be rushing away from each other at high speeds as a result of that initial explosion.

The renowned physicist Fred Hoyle derisively referred to this energy explosion as the "Big Bang," since he was sure that the universe was eternal.[8] The Big Bang theory states that the entire physical universe, all matter, energy, and the four dimensions of time and space, burst forth from this explosion.

Scientific theories about the origins of the universe took a quantum leap in 1965 when physicists Arno Penzias and Robert Wilson made a startling, serendipitous discovery. They were trying to calibrate a microwave detector for Bell Telephone Laboratories, but, much to their consternation, no matter where they aimed it, the detector kept picking up background noise. They tried cleaning the detector, then overhauled the electronic system, but they couldn't get rid of the noise. A series of studies indicated that this noise was filling the universe.

Professor P. J. E. Peebles at Princeton University explained to them that they had found the noise that resulted from the Big Bang. They then read an essay written by one of Friedmann's students which had predicted that remnants of the universe's explosion should be detectable in the form of weak microwave radiation of the type that Penzias and Wilson had discovered. These two men had discovered the echo of the explosion that brought the universe into being, and were awarded the Nobel Prize in 1978 for their findings. Steven Weinberg, a world-renowned physicist, called their findings "one of the most important scientific discoveries of the 20th century."[9]

By this time, scientists wanted an independent body to determine if the universe was eternal, because study after study was showing that it was not. Robert Jastrow, a great astrophysicist, was the director of NASA's Goddard Center for Space Studies. He was appointed the head of a research project that included mathematicians, astronomers, and physicists who wanted to prove the eternity of the world. After 15 years of research, Jastrow published NASA's report (1978). He shocked the public by concluding that the universe, rather than being eternal, probably came into being at a certain point in time. He wrote,

> This is an exceedingly strange development, unexpected by all but the theologians. They have always accepted the word of the Bible: "In the beginning, God created the heaven and the earth . . . ." For the scientist who has lived by his faith in the power of reason, the story ends like a bad dream. He has scaled the mountains of ignorance; he is about to conquer the highest peak; as he pulls himself over the final rock, he is greeted by a band of theologians who have been sitting there for centuries.[10]

Today, decades of scientific research support the idea that the universe came into being from nothing. The Big Bang theory, and no other, accounts for four main findings: the background noise found by Penzias and Wilson, the ratio of hydrogen to helium in the universe,[11] the expansion of the galaxies that Hubble observed, and the perfect black-body spectrum of the microwave background radiation as measured by the COBE (Cosmic Background Explorer) space satellite in 1989.[12] Scientific books and reams of articles have been written about the evidence that the universe came about in ways that are in harmony with the Torah's account of Creation.[13]

How Scientists Think the Universe Began

Renowned physicists today, such as Stephen Weinberg[14] and Stephen Hawking,[15] concur that nothing existed at a certain point in time, and then, all of a sudden, there was a moment of creation. The universe began with the explosion of a great ball of light/energy now generally known as the Big Bang. This enormous burst of concentrated energy became the source of all matter in the universe.[16] When this ball of light exploded, it brought into existence all of the laws of nature, time, space, and matter.[17]

This matter took the form of plasma, charged particles that trap light. A very short time after the Big Bang, there was intense light from the explosion, but it was trapped in this plasma so that although photons were given off, they were quickly reabsorbed. When this initial energy cooled very quickly, the plasma became atoms. Then the light shone through and radiation (light) dominated the early universe, as in Genesis:

And God said, "Let there be light, and there was light."[18]

Resistance to Theology

If a person came to a city, he would assume that people had built it—that it didn't simply spontaneously appear one day. Yet for thousands of years, scientists and philosophers were willing to believe that the complex universe in which we live had been here forever. Einstein resisted the idea of a created universe, even after there was abundant evidence to show that the world was not eternal. Today, many scientists such as Stephen Hawking admit, "The creation [of the universe] lies outside the scope of the presently known laws of physics,"[19] yet are not willing to attribute creation to God.

Chance and the Non-Created Universe

A world that has always been here has no moral plan, purpose, or meaning. If the world and people got here by chance, our job is simply to survive and do as we please. Unfortunately, history has shown that when people make their own rules about how best to live, they are prone to be self-serving. Ancient Greece and Rome, Nazi Germany, and other "enlightened" cultures had no qualms about enslaving people; killing babies, the elderly, and the sick; and glorifying sexual decadence. Most people think of ancient Greece and Rome as enlightened empires that gave us Western civilization, respect for human rights, and democracy. Yet it has been estimated that more than 25% of the people in the Roman empire and 30% in ancient Athens were enslaved. Slavery was so common in Rome that slaves far outnumbered citizens. As the Roman Republic expanded, they enslaved entire conquered populations.[20]

Ultimate Game of Hide and Seek

Genesis is constructed to lead us from the fact of creation to why God created it, for if He deliberately created a world—especially an incredibly complex world such as ours—He must have had a purpose for it and for us.

Judaism teaches that the functions of the world's masks of nature and materialism are to obscure their Source—to induce us to look for and find their Creator.[21] That is why the Hebrew word for world, *olam,* comes from the word *he'elem,* which means "hidden."

The rest of the Torah, and the oral traditions that have been passed down to us since the time of Moses, gives us detailed and practical answers to the questions, "Why did a Creator make this world, and how were we meant to use it?"[22]

Implications for Us
The Perfect Bull's-Eye

A man wanted to find out how a renowned archer always seemed to score a bull's-eye wherever he shot his arrows. Walking past an impressive series of ten arrows stuck in the center of each of ten targets, the man caught up with the archer and asked, "How do you manage to score a perfect bull's-eye each time you shoot?"

"Oh, it's easy," the archer replied. "First I shoot an arrow at the tree, then I paint a bull's-eye around it."

Instead of constructing a worldview based on what makes us comfortable, Genesis opens by telling us that God created a purposeful world so that we will live with His plan of meaning. One of our greatest challenges is to see life from His perspective, rather than from our own.

Notes
1. Genesis 1:1-2, 4.
2. Two-thirds of scientists who were surveyed in 1959 believed that the world was eternal! (Personal communication with physicist Gerald Schroeder.)
3. Hawking, Stephen, ed. *On the Shoulders of Giants: The Great Works of Physics and Astronomy.* Philadelphia, Running Press Book Publishers, 2004.
4. Einstein first wrote "On the Electrodynamics of Moving Bodies" in 1905. It was reprinted in H.A. Lorentz, A. Einstein, H. Minkowski, and W. H. Weyl, "The Principles of Relativity: A Collection of Original Papers on the Special Theory of Relativity." *Fortschritte der mathematischen Wissenschaften in Monographien,* Heft 2. Leipzig, 1922.
5. Jaki, Stanley. "From Scientific Cosmology to a Created Universe," in Roy Varghese: *Intellectuals Speak Out About God.* Chicago, Regnery Gateway Inc., 1984, p. 76.
6. Jastrow, Robert. *God and the Astronomers.* New York, Warner Books, 2000, p. 29.
7. Gamow, George. *Nature* (162), 1948, p. 680.
8. Hoyle, Fred. "A New Model for the Expanding Universes," *Monthly Notices of the Royal Astronomical Society* (108), 1948, p. 102.
9. Weinberg, Stephen. *The First Three Minutes.* London, Andre Deutsch and Fontana, 1977, p. 120.
10. Jastrow, Robert. *ibid.,* p. 125.
11. The Big Bang theory predicts that the universe would have consisted almost entirely of hydrogen and helium nuclei a few minutes after the initial explosion occurred. Their ratio, by mass, would have been 70-75% hydrogen and 25-30% helium. The fact that hydrogen and helium exist in these proportions in the universe today supports the Big Bang theory.
12. The Cosmic Background Explorer (COBE) was launched in November 1989 to see if there were minute differences in temperature across the background radiation of the universe that would indicate that the original expanding universe was not uniform and smooth, and that it could have given rise to galaxy clusters. COBE sent back information in April 1992 showing temperature differences of ten millionths of a degree. That information was consistent with the Big Bang theory.
13. For example, George Gamow, "The Origin of Elements and the Separation of Galaxies," *Physical Review* (74), 1948, p. 505. Gamow's ideas laid the foundation for our present understanding of big-bang nucleosynthesis. A number of books authored by physicists describe the origins of the universe in ways that are consistent with Creation: Stephen Weinberg, *The First Three Minutes.* London, Andre Deutsch and Fontana, 1977; Gerald Schroeder, *Genesis and the Big Bang,* New York, Bantam, 1990; Andrew Goldfinger, *Thinking about Creation,* Northvale, NJ, Jason Aronson, 1999; Nathan Aviezer, *In the Beginning: Biblical Creation and Science,* Hoboken, NJ, Ktav, 1990; and Nathan Aviezer, *Fossils and Faith,* Hoboken, NJ, Ktav, 2001.

14. Weinberg, Stephen. *op. cit.*
15. Hawking, Stephen. *A Brief History of Time.* New York, Bantam Books, 1988. Hawking is one of the best-known physicists today; his popular book on cosmology has sold over 15 million copies!
16. This is consistent with Einstein's famous equation, $E=mc^2$, where a small amount of energy results in a huge amount of matter.
17. Wheeler, John. *Geons, Black Holes and Quantum Foam.* New York, Norton, 1998, p. 350.
18. Genesis 1:3-4.
19. Hawking, Stephen. *The Large Scale Structure of Space-Time.* Cambridge University Press, 1973, p. 364.
20. http://en.wikipedia.org/wiki/History_of_slavery
21. This idea is beautifully discussed in Akiva Tatz, *Worldmask.* Jerusalem, Targum, 1995.
22. Luzzatto, Moshe Chaim, *The Way of God,* discusses topics such as the purpose of life and how people can fulfill their purposes here.

Science and Creation

Inasmuch as Genesis describes the Creation of the world in a way that seems similar to many ancient myths, intelligent people often dismiss the Biblical account out of hand.[1] While the Torah's purpose is not to discuss cosmology, but rather to teach how God wants us to live, the description is also consistent with what scientists tell us about the creation of the universe.

The First Day

Some accept the idea of a Big Bang, yet scoff at the Biblical idea that a universe came into being in one day. They assume that an event of such extraordinary magnitude must have taken billions of years to occur! Yet, physicists believe that the infant universe was so hot that it took a *mere three minutes* for the building blocks of every material that exists in the entire universe to come into being![2]

People once thought it ludicrous that ancient Jewish mystical books said that God created the world using letters. We now take for granted that all life is based on DNA, which in turn is made up of base pairs known by their initials, A, C, G, and T. If we accept that physical life is composed of "letters," it no longer seems so ludicrous that the spiritual basis of life is also composed of "letters."

To see how other ideas in the Genesis Creation story make sense, we have to know a lot of science. For example, the first chapter of Genesis tells how the world was created in ways that seem simplistic at face value, yet are consistent with geological, archaeological, and scientific findings.[3] We will mention just a few of them as we look at some Biblical verses.

The Second Day

> *And God said, "Let there be a firmament in the midst of the water, and let it divide between water and water." And God made the firmament, and divided between the water which is under the firmament and the water which is over the firmament, and it was so. And God called the firmament "heavens," and there was evening and there was morning a second day.*[4]

At first glance, many people think that these verses refer to a primitive God making rain clouds and oceans, yet there is far more here than meets the eye. The firmament referred to here is what we call "outer space," and the lower waters are bodies of water on earth such as lakes and oceans. What, then, are the "upper waters?"

Scientific research[5] has revealed that there is much more water in the far regions of outer space than on planet Earth. The outer planets in our solar system, from Mars to Neptune, and their large moons, have layers of frozen water that are hundreds and even thousands of miles thick. Yet most of the upper water is in comets, which are formed from ice, dust, and other particles. It is quite amazing that a small comet contains around a billion tons of ice, and a large comet has many times more! Even more astounding, our solar system has a comet "reservoir" at its edge that alone has a trillion comets in it![6] If all of the comets in our solar system were to melt, they would contain many times more water than Earth's oceans.[7]

The Third Day

> *And God said, "Let the water under the heavens be gathered to one place, and the dry land will be seen," and it was so. And God called the dry land "land" and the gathering of the water He called "seas." And God saw that it was good. And God said, "Let the earth sprout vegetation, grasses that produce seed, fruit trees making fruit according to its kind, whose seed is in it upon the*

earth, and it was so. And the earth produced vegetation, grass-making seed according to its kind, and fruit-making trees, with seeds in it according to its kind, and God saw that it was good. And there was evening and there was morning a third day.[8]

Although today the earth has seven continents separated by vast oceans, that was not always the case. Geologists believe that warm water covered most of the earth during the Devonian period.[9] It was followed by the Permian period,[10] when a severe ice age occurred. Much seawater froze into polar ice caps, causing the oceans to recede, many large seas to disappear, and much dry land to appear. At that time, the earth had one continent, which geologists call Pangea, a vast ocean, and huge ice caps, especially near the South Pole.[11] This is consistent with Genesis describing, "Let the water . . . be gathered to one place, and the dry land will be seen." An area near the South Pole was the "one place" where these waters gathered.[12]

This Permian ice age killed as much as 90% of all living species. At that time, there was mostly primitive marine life that lived in warm, shallow water.[13] Yet, later in the Permian period, modern-type green plants first spread about the face of the earth. (Prior to this time, there was only primitive flora that lay people would not recognize as plants.) Genesis tells us that God made vegetation after the receding water revealed dry land, and this is consistent with what scientists have found.

The Fourth Day

And God said, "Let there be lights in the firmament of the heavens, to divide the day from the night, and to be for signs, and seasons, and days and years. And they will be for lights in the firmament of the heaven to cast light on the earth," and it was so. And God made the two great lights, the big light to rule the day and the small light to rule the night, and the stars. And God gave them in the firmament of the heaven to light up the earth, and to rule in the day and night, and to separate the light from the darkness. And

God saw that it was good. And there was evening and there was morning a fourth day.[14]

Scientific truth is often stranger than fiction. We take for granted that the sun and moon have always been here, with days of 24 hours and years of 365 days. Yet geologists tell us that in the middle of the Paleozoic era,[15] days had only 21 hours and there were more than 400 days in a year. Moreover, in the northern hemisphere winter started in June and summer started in December, exactly the opposite of what occurs now. It was the moon's gravitational pull and the fixing of the relative alignments of the sun, moon, and earth that caused the present 24-hour days and 365-day years.

The moon's pull on the earth affects the earth's orbit around the sun such that we have had ten ice ages, each followed by a warm period. The relatively mild climate that we now enjoy has allowed people to develop culturally, intellectually, and technologically more than at any other time in history.

Anthropic Principle

Some people think that the world could have come into being by chance. Not only does scientific evidence indicate that the world was created in a way that is consistent with Genesis' descriptions, it is consistent with what scientists call the "anthropic principle." The universe seems to have been created with human beings in mind. Planet Earth "just happens" to be exactly the right distance from the sun to allow humans to live here. Shortly after they were formed, Earth, Venus, and Mars all had comparable amounts of surface water. When Venus heated up, its water evaporated, and when Mars cooled, its water froze. Were Earth just a tad closer to the sun, it would have been so hot that the waters here would have evaporated as they did on Venus, and we couldn't have survived in the fierce heat. Were Earth just a tad farther from the sun, the water would have frozen into ice, as it did on Mars. There are many extremely unusual occurrences that affect Earth's climate, atmosphere, and other conditions to make Earth the only planet in our solar system where humans can survive.[16] To some, these events are merely a series of natural coincidences.

Genesis tells us that they were engineered by a God Who wanted us to be here.

Implications for Us

In the staggering series of improbable events that caused the creation of our solar system; the uniqueness of planet Earth, its moon, climate, and living conditions; and the existence of human beings, we can discern a divine handprint. Judaism teaches that our Creator did all this because He loved us so much that He created a world in which we could be beneficiaries of His goodness. It is up to us to live in a way that we show our Creator that all of His efforts were worthwhile.

Notes

1. According to Genesis and Jewish tradition, the world was created in only six days, some 5,768 years ago, while according to scientists, it is billions of years old. There are many approaches to resolve this discrepancy. For example, *Akeidat Yitzchak*, the Sforno, and Nachmanides wrote that the six "days" of creation refer to periods of time, not 24-hour days. Since the sun wasn't created until the fourth day, there were no 24-hour "days" of light and dark prior to that time. Other scholars point to the fact that events at the beginning of the universe took place much more quickly than they would occur now. What took a fraction of a second to occur then would take millions of years to take place now. Gerald Schroeder, in *Genesis and the Big Bang* (New York, Bantam, 1990) reconciles how the world could have been created in both six days and billions of years, depending upon the frame of reference from which one measures time. He also shows how the various periods of geologic time can be simultaneously understood from both the scientific and Biblical ways of measuring them.

2. Weinberg, Stephen. *The First Three Minutes.* London, Andre Deutsch and Fontana, 1977. This Nobel prize-winner describes the origins of the universe in this book.

3. See Gerald Schroeder, *Genesis and the Big Bang,* New York, Bantam, 1990; Andrew Goldfinger, *Thinking about Creation*, Northvale, NJ, Jason Aronson, 1999; Nathan Aviezer, *In the Beginning: Biblical Creation and Science,* Hoboken, NJ, Ktav, 1990; and Nathan Aviezer, *Fossils and Faith*, Hoboken, NJ, Ktav, 2001.

4. Genesis 1:6-8.

5. These bodies of ice in outer space are discussed in J. Audouze et al., eds., *The Cambridge Atlas of Astronomy.* Cambridge University Press, 1985, pp. 212-219.

6. Aviezer, Nathan. *In the Beginning*, Hoboken, NJ, Ktav, 1990, p. 22. This is known as the Oort cloud, named after its discoverer.

7. *Ibid.*

8. Genesis 1:9-13.

9. Scientists date the Devonian period to 408 million until 360 million years ago. It was a time of great tectonic activity.

10. Scientists call the last period of geologic time in the Paleozoic Era the Permian period. They date it from 290 million years ago until 250 million years ago.

11. Nathan Aviezer, *op. cit*, p. 33. Pangea eventually broke up and its pieces drifted to where today's continents are.

12. Smith, D. G. (ed.). *The Cambridge Encyclopedia of Earth Sciences.* Cambridge University Press, 1981, p. 299.

13. Eldredge, Niles. *Time Frames.* New York, Simon and Schuster, 1985, p.39.

14. Genesis 1:14-19.

15. Scientists date this era to 570 million to 240 million years ago.

16. Scientists call this the "Goldilocks problem of climatology"!

Evolution

Creation vs. Random Mutation

Thanks to the famous Scopes trial, many people think that only uneducated people can believe in Genesis' accounts of the origin of species. On the other hand, Darwin's theory of evolution has become so accepted by the public that attacking his theory is almost like attacking democracy! So, before we examine Darwin's ideas, let's see what Genesis has to say about how life came to inhabit the earth:

> *And God said, "Let the water swarm with swarming creatures that are alive, and birds that fly over the earth, across the firmament of the heaven." And God created the great sea-creatures, and all the living creatures that crawl, that swarm in the water according to their kind, and all winged birds according to their kind, and God saw that it was good. And God blessed them saying, "Be fruitful and multiply, and fill the water in the seas, and the birds shall increase on the earth." And there was evening and there was morning a fifth day.*
>
> *And God said, "Let the earth bring forth living beings according to each's kind—beasts, and creeping [animals], and life of the earth according to its kind," and it was so. And God made the animals of the earth according to their kind, and the beasts according to their kind, and all that creeps on the earth according to its kind. And God saw that it was good.*
>
> *And God created the man in His image, in the image of God He created him, male and female He created them.[1]*

In 1859, Darwin proposed some new ideas in *The Origin of Species:* lower, simpler animals such as sea creatures evolved into higher species such as man. Both Genesis and Darwin agree on the general order that each species came into being: first sea life, then fowl, then reptiles, then land-based animals, and finally humans.

While Darwin believed that more-developed species such as humans came into being by a random mutation process, followed by natural selection, Genesis stresses that God created each group of animals as distinct species, with man as a singular entity with a unique, divine soul.

Purposefulness vs. Chance

On the first day of creation, according to Rashi (the medieval Jewish commentator), God created the potential for each species to exist. Each successive day of creation, He put a variety of distinct species on earth.[2] This account disputes the idea that all life forms arose by chance.

Genesis says that God created all non-human species in masses. They then developed according to His laws of nature.[3] *The Origin of Species* proposes that species evolved via a random process from lower into higher forms of life as natural selection occurred over many millions of years. Thus, the tiniest specks of life eventually gave rise to human beings. Scientists believed that this metamorphosis occurred over millions of years as each generation had small mutations that allowed them to adapt to their environment better than the prior generation had.[4] These "good" mutations kept being passed to their descendants until new species, which were more developed than the earlier species, came into being.

What Is a Species?

To test whether Darwin was correct, we need to first investigate the foundation of his ideas. For example, what is a species? Most of us learned in high school biology that a species is a group of animals that can breed with one another, yet the truth is not so simple.[5] Scientists have discovered that as many as 20-25% of some species interbreed with one another and bear fertile offspring![6]

Evolutionary biologists themselves cannot agree about what a species is or what has evolved. As one biologist said, "Species do not have an objective reality in nature. . . . We have embarrassingly little evidence for some widely held notions in systematics and evolutionary biology."[7]

Directed Mutations

A second foundation of Darwin's theory is that mutations always occur randomly, and then natural selection, which isn't random, causes animals with helpful mutations to survive over time. In 1988, experiments done using bacteria at Harvard University showed that mutations are sometimes directed, not random. A special strain of bacteria that could not digest milk sugar was given only milk sugar. The researchers expected the bacteria to stay inert. Instead, some bacteria mutated their gene to make the enzyme that could digest milk sugar, and they then thrived and multiplied. The amazed scientists remarked, "That such events ever occur seems almost unbelievable. . . . The main purpose of this paper is to show how insecure is our belief in the randomness of mutations."[8]

Years later, an article in *Scientific American* proclaimed, "New findings suggest that mutation is more complicated than anyone thought. . . . This radical proposal collided head-on with the sacrosanct principle that mutations occur at a rate that is completely unrelated to whatever consequences they might have."[9]

Progression Confusion

Leading evolutionary biologists cannot even agree about the most basic ideas of evolution. For example, Richard Dawkins at Oxford University believes that evolution has progressed in the animal kingdom, while Stephen Jay Gould of Harvard University doesn't. These two respected scientists disagree about the fundamentals of evolution itself![10]

Missing Links

Darwin also said that primitive species continually evolve into ones that are more sophisticated (macroevolution). If this were true, we would expect to find fossils showing intermediate stages of this species-to-species evolution, yet archaeologists have never found fossils that bridge one species to another! For example, Neanderthal man shows up in the fossil record then abruptly disappears. Since then, only modern man appears in the fossil record, with no intermediary form of human found between Neanderthal man and modern man. Notes Professor Stephen Stanley of Johns Hopkins University, a leading authority on human fossils, "Out of nowhere [modern man] appeared in the fossil record with particular features that are utterly unpredictable on the basis of what preceded them."[11]

Calamity-Based Evolution

Moreover, fossils appear in a bizarre pattern: Certain animals existed for many years, then a calamity suddenly occurred. Soon afterward, different species suddenly came into being.[12] Scientists currently believe that cataclysmic events have continually caused species to become extinct, regardless of whether or not the species were "fit."[13]

Why Fossil Records Get Tossed

Fossil records are consistent with Genesis' account that God progressively created different species after their kind and do not support Darwin's theory that lower forms of life gradually evolved into higher forms of life. Nevertheless, Darwin's theory is still taught in most high schools, universities, and natural history museums and is publicized as if it were correct because the alternative—that God created the world—has disturbing moral implications for secularists.

Famous Paleontological Frauds

People would like to think that scientists are objective observers and interpreters of information, yet history has shown that this is often not the case. We have already seen how Einstein and other physicists let their secular beliefs bias their work. Unfortunately, world-renowned paleontologists have been notoriously non-objective, even deceptive, about human origins. **They have perpetrated numerous hoaxes that scientists accepted uncritically for up to 40 years!**

For example, a famous French paleontologist, Marcellin Boule, concocted the depiction of Neanderthal man as a crude, savage, long-armed, ape-like, stupid brute. Responded Niles Eldredge, a leading paleontologist, "Every feature Boule stressed in his analysis can be shown to have no basis in fact. . . . Boule's authority was so close to

27

absolute that his conclusions strongly affected paleontological thinking for several decades."[14]

Piltdown man, whose skull and jaw were "found" between 1912 and 1916, was another famous fraud. "From 1912-1953, every scientific reference book and encyclopedia informed its readers of the great importance of Piltdown Man in establishing the evolutionary history of Modern Man."[15] The three greatest British paleontologists of the 1920s and 1930s all agreed that Piltdown man was our earliest direct ancestor. It took 20 or 30 years to show that the Piltdown skull was from a contemporary human and the jaw was from a "touched-up" contemporary orangutan that made the forgery look more authentic.[16]

According to David Pilbeam, a Harvard University professor and modern authority on human origins, "Our theories have often said far more about the theorists than . . . about what actually happened. . . . Virtually all our theories . . . were fossil-free and in some cases even fossil-proof. . . . Many evolutionary schemes were in fact dominated by theoretical assumptions that were largely divorced from data derived from fossils."[17]

Should We Believe Darwin's Theories?

Physical Evolution: Although evolutionary theory sounds good from a physical point of view, Darwin's theories are not as unassailable as many would like us to believe. People should know that despite much hypothesizing, there is *no scientific evidence* to support Darwin's idea that humans are glorified apes, the product of an evolutionary chain that started with simple forms of life that led to higher forms of life. The Creator could have used Darwinian-type evolution to achieve His goals. It is the idea of random evolution rather than directed evolution that is theologically problematic. From a scientific point of view, it is untenable to say that life randomly evolved as it exists today. It can be shown statistically that the amount of time that scientists claim that Earth has existed is not long enough for even the most rudimentary aspects of life to have evolved by chance.[18] For example, a Yale professor of physics, Harold Morowitz, calculated the amount of time it could optimistically take a bacterium to evolve from a primordial bath of chemicals at more than 15 billion years! Scientists believe the entire universe came into existence 15 billion years ago and that life on earth began only 4.5 billion years ago.

Genesis rejects the core of the idea that randomness and not a Creator brought animals and people into the world. Rather, Genesis teaches that the Almighty deliberately created each original species, in the order generally accepted by scientists, with people being the most sublime creation of all:

The Lord God formed the person from the dust of the ground, and He breathed into his nose a soul of life, and the person was a living creature.[19]

Spiritual Evolution: Darwin's theory also fails to explain the evolution of our essence. Granted, people are genetically and physically similar to animals. Like us, animals may communicate, have impressive family and social networks, and use tools. Yet we have free will to be moral or immoral; animals don't. Animals rely on their instincts to guide them; we are to spiritually elevate our animalistic instincts by channeling them in ways that the Almighty bids us to. Animals don't strive to improve themselves and make the world a better place. We are supposed to do both.

It is our spiritual essence—our divine soul—that distinguishes us from all other forms of life. When we rise above our animalistic and egocentric drives, we can then identify with our soul's lofty purpose. Scientists will never find fossilized souls, yet that is what makes us special!

Implications for Us

It is a pity that some religious people view science as antithetical to religion or that scientists view religion as antithetical to science. Scientists largely reject the possibility of a Created world because it means they will have to act morally. Such scientists are not willing to curtail living as they please in exchange for a life of great meaning. Scientists could be more objective in their science and live more meaningfully were they only willing to conduct themselves as the Creator wants instead of deciding that He can't exist because if He did, they couldn't live as they please.

For centuries, many Christians have believed that science and the Bible are incompatible. By contrast, rabbis of the Mishna and Talmud were well versed in the science of their times, and their discussions in these books incorporate great knowledge of astronomy and biology. For example, they knew how to calculate the exact length of a solar year and adjust the lunar calendar to coordinate with the solar one for thousands of years to come. They discussed hereditary diseases such as hemophilia, biological anomalies, and reproductive physiology. They had rules for determining when a human being had died, how to assess whether a dead animal had an internal injury or illness that would have been lethal, and were aware of nutrition and medicinal healing. Medieval Jewish scholars such as Maimonides and Nachmanides were physicians. They studied science, and Maimonides wrote extensively about it in his treatises. Today, leading rabbis study the cutting edge of science to learn how to apply these ideas to medical ethics, long-distance and space travel, agriculture, laws of kashrut (foods that Jews may eat), reproductive endocrinology, and so on. Perhaps if people understood the importance of integrating science and religion, they would live more meaningfully.

The more science we know, the more we can marvel at the complex universe that God created. Science can help us understand the "hows" of the universe; the Torah can help us understand its "whys." Science can explain what is; the Torah can teach us how to spiritually refine what is by using the physical world in the ways that its Creator intended. The more we study science, the more we can appreciate how everything in the universe is part of a divine plan, with a divine purpose waiting to be fulfilled.

Notes

1. Genesis 1:20-27.
2. Rashi on Genesis 1:14; 1:24, and 2:4.
3. There were, of course, times when He intervened in nature by causing cataclysmic events such as the Great Flood.
4. Darwin called this process "natural selection." Herbert Spencer termed it "survival of the fittest," a phrase that is still used by many lay people.
5. See, for example, the college textbook by E.P. Solomon, L.R. Berg, D.W. Martin, and C. Villee (eds.), *Biology*, 4th ed. New York, Harcourt Brace, 1996, p. 434.
6. According to one scientist, 25% of UK flora hybridize, 75% of British duck species and all four of their game birds hybridize in the wild. "Animals display phylogenetic hotspots of natural hybridization that greatly exceed the 25% rate per species for vascular plants." James Mallett, "Hybridization as an Invasion of the Genome," *Trends in Ecology and Evolution* (20)5, May 2005, p. 230.
7. See Peter Raven, "Modern aspects of the biological species in plants." In K. Iwatsuki (ed.), *Modern Aspects of Species* (42), Tokyo, Tokyo Press, 1988, pp. 11-29.
8. Cairns, John, J. Overbaugh, and S. Miller, "The Origin of Mutants," *Nature* (335), 1988, pp. 142-145.
9. "In Focus," *Scientific American*, September 1997, p. 9.
10. See, for example, Jerry Coyne, Nicholas Barton, and Michael Turelli, "Perspective: A Critique of Sewall Wright's Shifting Balance Theory of Evolution," *Evolution* (51)3, June 1997, p. 1015.
11. Stanley, S. M. *The New Evolutionary Timetable.* New York, Basic Books, 1981, p. 151.
12. For example, the Alvarez theory of dinosaur extinction states that dinosaurs once roamed the earth and were the "fittest" creatures of their time. They became extinct moments after an asteroid struck the earth, creating a dust cloud and "nuclear winter" that annihilated these animals. Fossils show that dinosaurs underwent mass destruction all at once.
13. *Ibid.*
14. Eldredge, Niles. *The Myths of Human Evolution.* New York, Columbia University Press, 1982, p. 76.
15. Aviezer, Nathan. "Misreading the Fossils: The Dark Side of Evolutionary Biology," *Jewish Action* 58(2), Winter 1997, p. 63.
16. Stringer, Chris, and J. S. Weiner. *The Piltdown Forgery.* Oxford University Press, 2004.
17. Pilbeam, David. "Current Argument on Early Man." In *Major Trends in Evolution*, ed. L.K. Konigson. London, Pergamon Press, 1980, pp. 262, 267.
18. Schroeder, Gerald. *Genesis and the Big Bang.* New York, Bantam Books, 1990, pp. 110-115. For example, Schroeder shows how the feed stocks of random reactions would have required billions of times more carbon than exists in the entire universe to make proteins that are similar in animals and humans, and an extraordinary amount of time longer than has existed since

the Big Bang occurred. The evolution of the human eye or other organs likewise would have required far more time than has passed.

19. Genesis 2:7.

Two Creation Stories

Genesis presents two slightly different accounts of man's creation. The first account refers to the Almighty as *Elo-him* (God), the second and later chapters call Him *Ado-nai Elo-him* (Lord God). Is this evidence that two different authors wrote these stories, as "Biblical critics" would have you believe? Let's see how discrepancies between the two versions actually offer new understandings of our role in the world.

The first creation story begins with the world's creation and ends with the creation of people:

> *And God said, "Let us make man in our image and likeness. And they will rule the fish of the sea, and the birds of the heaven, and the beasts, and over all the earth, and every crawling thing that crawls on the earth." And God created the man in His image, in the image of God He created him, male and female He created them. And God blessed them, and God said to them, "Be fruitful and multiply, and fill up the earth, and conquer it, and rule the fish of the sea, and the birds of the heaven, and all the animals that crawl on the earth."*
>
> *And God said, "Behold, I gave you all the grass that has seed that is on the face of the earth, and every tree that contains tree fruit with seeds, for you it shall be food."¹*

The second creation story portrays only the creation of people:

> *And the Lord God formed the person [from] dust of the ground, and He blew in his nose a soul of life and the person was a living being. And the Lord God planted a garden in Eden to the east, and he put the person there whom He had formed. And the Lord God made grow from the earth every tree that was pleasant to look at and good*

for eating, and the tree of life was in the midst of the garden, and the tree of knowledge of good and bad. . . .[2]

Having created man as described in Chapter 1, God in Chapter 2 charges the first person with his spiritual task. In Chapter 3, man disobeys God.

What's in a Name?

Bible critics claim the names *Ado-nai* and *Elo-him* represent two different gods that the ancient Jews worshipped. This is akin to the following argument: William Smith is a married man with a business. His parents call him Billy, his wife calls him Honey, his son calls him Dad, his friends call him Bill, his employees call him Mr. Smith, and telemarketers call him William. Therefore, William Smith must be six different people because he has six different names!

The Torah teaches that there is only one invisible God and that His various names express nuances of how we experience Him. *Elo-him* refers to God when we experience Him meting out justice or ruling nature;[3] *Ado-nai* refers to God when we experience Him as loving. The first story uses only the name *Elo-him* because it describes how the Master of nature created an ideal world that was supposed to follow rules of strict justice. Thus, Genesis uses the nature-ruling term Elo-him when God creates the world and the loving term Ado-nai Elo-him when God creates or interacts with man.

Implications for Us

Using the name Ado-nai Elo-him in only the second creation account helps us appreciate how God reveals different aspects of Himself to maintain an ongoing relationship with us. Our Creator wanted to express His love for us by putting us in a world where we could do things to draw close to Him. Every time that we fulfill a divine commandment, we create intimacy with the Almighty. Every time that we disobey His will, we create distance and spiritually harm the world that He made for us—a place where we could create a loving closeness with Him.

In the second Creation story, the first person was told not to eat of the fruit of a certain tree. Had he obeyed, he would have fulfilled his spiritual purpose and deepened his trust in, and closeness with, his Creator. However, he didn't trust God. He ate the forbidden fruit, relying on his own instincts to tell him that he knew better than God what was best for him. Yet instead of destroying man on the spot (as strict justice would require), the Almighty gave him a chance to repent, be punished, and continue having a relationship with Him.

Since we are human and often fail, God tempered His system of justice to make allowances for our shortcomings. Instead of killing us upon commission of a sin, He gives us opportunities to repent and to draw close to Him once more.

The second story uses God's name Ado-nai Elo-him to remind us that our Creator loves us so profoundly that He altered His plan for Creation to accommodate our imperfections! When justice is necessary, it is usually done in as loving and kind a way as possible.

Notes
1. Genesis 1:2-2:6.
2. Genesis 2:7-9.
3. Hebrew numerology, known as *gematria*, alludes to this. *Gematria* is a type of Biblical interpretation that uses the numerical value of Hebrew letters to uncover deeper messages in the words. Each Hebrew letter has a numerical value: the first letter, *aleph*, equals one, the second letter, *bet*, equals two, and so on. The numerical value of the letters in the world Elo-him equal 86 and the value of the letters in the Hebrew word for nature, *hateva*, also equal 86. The equivalence teaches us that nature is nothing more than the manifestation of God's will.

A New Look at Self-Worth

Judaism teaches that we can learn personal lessons from the Torah's descriptions of Creation and from the way that God designed the universe. Even the laws of science have something to teach us about ourselves and our relationship with the Almighty. We will soon see how these emphasize our potential worth in His eyes.

After telling us how God created the world, Genesis says:

> *These are the stories of the heaven and the earth when they were created on the day that the Lord God made earth and heaven. And every tree of the field before it was in the ground, and every grass of the field before it sprouted, because the Lord God didn't make it rain on the ground, and there was no person to work the earth.*[1]

After creating the entire universe, the show couldn't "open" until the Almighty created man! It is as if a huge extravaganza were waiting for the star to emerge from behind the curtain and take center stage. God could certainly have made the trees and grass flourish without humanity, but He chose not to. He deliberately left the world incomplete because He wanted us to appreciate our centrality in spiritually perfecting His world.

It would be easy for us to feel unimportant, as mere specks that randomly appeared in a vast, incomprehensibly complex universe. The opening chapters of Genesis remind us that God deliberately created us, that we were the climax of Creation, and that we are indispensable to His world.

Physicists have discovered many principles governing the universe that defy our common sense. It is remarkable that the Almighty embedded ideas in the laws of physics that teach us about our unique worth, even as they make us feel humbled by, and in awe of, our Creator's greatness.

For example, in the field of relativity, a classic paradox has identical twins going their separate ways. One decides to become an astronaut, and, at the age of 30, he rockets off into space at nearly the speed of light. The other stays on Earth. The astronaut returns to Earth after his watch tells him that two years have elapsed. When he greets his brother, the astronaut is 32 years old, yet his identical twin is 72 years old! How is that possible? Time elapses differently depending upon how fast one is traveling.

It has actually been proven that time moves slower when matter travels at high speeds. One traveler took a plane trip with an extremely accurate "atomic clock," while an identical atomic clock stayed in the lab. When the "traveling" clock came back, it had fallen behind the "couch potato" clock, just as Einstein's theory of relativity predicted it should.[2]

Quantum physics says that *a given particle is everywhere and nowhere at the same time until we observe where it actually is.* Only once we observe and measure the particle does our action cause the particle to really exist in only one place.[3] The renowned mathematical physicist John von Neumann concluded[4] that it is the mind of someone observing the world that makes the world real.[5]

There are many possibilities of where atoms can be in the world. "Reality" occurs when only one possibility exists instead of an infinite number of possibilities. As bizarre as it sounds, experiments[6] have shown that *reality does not truly happen until we observe it*! We can learn from this that God designed a world that requires our interacting with it to be real.

Implications for Us

These laws of physics have profound theological implications: The complex, vast universe that God made only becomes real[7] when we observe and interact with it! Our Creator has made a universe that crucially depends on a human observer for its existence. Therefore, the idea that humanity is the pinnacle of Creation is not merely a nice idea, but the cornerstone of the world's existence. The Torah bids us to fulfill the world's purpose not only by making it real, but also by living in such a way that we, and the world around us, have meaning.

Notes

1. Genesis 2:4-5.
2. Allen, Jesse. http://imagine.gsfc.nasa.gov/docs/ask_astro/answers/970902c.html
3. Richard Feynman, a Nobel laureate in physics, showed that photons travel between point A and point B taking *all* possible paths at the same time. Once a human being measures where a photon is, we limit it to a specific path and it doesn't go any other way.
4. He wrote the most influential book about quantum theory ever written.
5. Physicist Fritz London said, "It is only the consciousness of an 'I' who can, by virtue of his observation, set up a new objectivity."
6. Physics students learn about the classic thought experiment called "Schroedinger's cat." It posits that there is a cat in a box, and the student has to determine if the cat is alive or dead. Quantum mechanics says that it is actually both alive and dead at the same time! Only by opening the box does the observer force it into one of two possible states, and that observation is what creates the real world! This phenomenon can actually be observed at the microscopic level.

   If this disturbs you, then you are in good company! Even Einstein was disturbed by the bizarre way the physical world operates. It defies human logic.
7. As Supreme Court justice Potter Stewart once said when asked to explain "hard-core" pornography, or what is obscene, "I shall not today attempt further to define the kinds of material I understand to be embraced . . . [b]ut I know it when I see it." (Jacobellis v. Ohio, 378 U.S. 184, 197, 1964). In order to settle on a practical definition, we will define physical "reality" in a similar fashion.

Evening and Morning

One way that we bring meaning to the world is by living in it as God has asked us to.

We make choices every day that can detract from the world's spiritual wholesomeness, that can be neutral, or that can connect the world to its Creator. We have constant opportunities to think, speak, and act in ways that bring us (and the world) closer to the Almighty or that distance us from Him. When we see God's hand in nature while watching a waterfall, for instance, we are connecting the waterfall and ourselves to our mutual Source. When we speak kindly to someone, we imitate our Parent in Heaven. When we give food to someone who is hungry, we have used the physical world for a purpose for which the Almighty designed it.

At the end of almost every day of Creation, the Torah says that God observed His world and saw that "it was good." Each of these divine conclusions is followed by the phrase "And there was evening [*erev*], and there was morning [*boker*]" that day.

Actually, the words *erev* and *boker* mean more than "evening" and "morning." *Erev* also means "mixture," while *boker* means "clarity." One of the laws of physics is that entropy, a scientific measure of disorder, always increases. The fact that there was increasing order during Creation was solely due to the will of the Creator.

Some traditional Jewish commentators say that the days of Creation do not refer to 24-hour periods but rather to periods of Creation that had some chaos in them, which the Almighty decreased by making the world more orderly. "It was good" refers to the resulting order.[1]

Implications for Us

God wants us to be like Him. We do this by bringing order and spiritual clarity to a confusing, morally chaotic world. When we see each day's opportunities and use them to bring meaning and spiritual purpose to our lives and to the world around us, the world becomes a good place.

We can be God's partners in creating an orderly and meaningful world out of the chaos that surrounds us by expressing our inner divinity. We can start by following the Torah's prescriptions for how to live. In addition, we need to work on our character defects and make our lives models for others to imitate. Finally, when we see or hear about injustice, social problems, and the like, we should do what we can to alleviate them.

Notes

1. This is Onkelos' interpretation. He was a traditional Jewish commentator who lived approximately 1,900 years ago. He wrote an Aramaic commentary on the Torah that is still read today. The Talmud (*Gittin* 56b) says that Onkelos was the Roman emperor Titus' nephew. Titus was responsible for destroying the Second Temple and Jerusalem, and exiled the Jews from Israel in the year 70 CE.

The Uniqueness of People

Judaism teaches that God designed every detail of creation and of the universe with a spiritual message behind it. For example, the fact that God created all other forms of life before He created people teaches us not to be arrogant. After all, if the mosquito preceded us, how can we think that we're such hot stuff?! On the other hand, if all else preceded us, we must be the crowning achievement of God's world.

God originally created only one person, while the animals were created in swarms. If people were the climax of Creation, we might think that it was only worthwhile to make a world for the sake of many human beings, created in swarms just like animals. We instead learn that it was worthwhile for the Almighty to make the entire world for the sake of just one human being. What a boost to our self-esteem!

People sometimes wonder if all the world's people really did descend from Adam and Eve. DNA testing of many people has shown that all people descended from one woman, whom scientists call "Eve."[1]

Implications for Us

We can learn from this detail of creation never to lord our lineage over anyone else, since we all come from the same, original parents. It is not our genes that make us important; it is what we do with what the Almighty gave us that makes us special.

If the Almighty gives some people fewer talents, resources, or physical gifts than others have, they will still find themselves in circumstances that will allow them to fulfill their spiritual purpose with what they have.

We often judge ourselves, and others, based on what we have rather than on what we have become. Being moral and making spiritual contributions to the world doesn't require being beautiful, rich, smart, physically healthy, or talented. In fact, sometimes people who have the least materially are the most appreciative and try the hardest to make the most of their opportunities.

Comparing ourselves materially, intellectually, or physically to others is useless. We each have unique endowments and challenges because our Creator wants us to make spiritual contributions to the world that no one else can make. In God's world, everyone can compete for the same prize—loving intimacy with our Creator—and no one need lose. Our life's task is to try our best to shine our unique spiritual light into the world by perfecting our souls and the world to the best of our abilities.

Notes
1. Cann, Rebecca. Allan Wilson, and Mark Stoneking, "Mitochondrial DNA and Human Evolution." *Nature* (325), 1987, pp. 31-36.

The Right Stuff

People often think that our bodies and the material world are what is important. Judaism teaches that both are mere vehicles for helping the soul fulfill its purpose. For example, Genesis says that God made the first person from "the dust of the earth [*adamah*], and He breathed into his nose a soul of life, and the person was a living creature."[1]

If the Almighty wanted to stress the importance of the body, He could have made us from gold or silver. Likewise, if the body were important in its own right, it wouldn't need a soul from God to vivify it.

One Midrash (homiletical story) asserts that Adam was created from the dust of all the earth, while another says that he was formed using dust from the future location of the altar in Jerusalem's holy Temple. The idea that Adam was made from dust everywhere implies that the entire world's existence depended on Adam's using it the way that God intended. It also teaches that he had within him all of the qualities and potentials of people who would exist everywhere in the world. People around the world should identify with the purpose for which God created Adam—namely, to recognize the Creator of the physical world and to use the world to do His bidding.

The Midrash that says Adam was made from the dust of the altar implies that Adam could make his physical being Godly. By sacrificing his desires to those of his Creator, and doing only what His Creator told him was right, Adam could elevate the physical world and spiritually perfect it. He could use his body to bring Heaven to earth.[2]

A body that is made of dust is insignificant and has little inherent value. The actual materials that make up a body are almost worthless. Bodies are incredibly important, though, insofar as they allow our souls to realize their potential. In this regard, they are priceless.

Adam did not use his body to live up to his spiritual calling. Instead, he brought death into the world. From then on, bodies would die and their souls would pass into an eternal afterlife. There, each soul goes through a life review and sees what its body's spiritual challenges were and how the person responded to the challenges that God sent his or her way.

People who gave up trying to follow God's plan because they felt that their moral challenges were insurmountable will see that their challenges were really no more difficult than crossing over a thread. Righteous people who disciplined themselves to follow God's plans will see that their actual challenges were like looming mountains, yet they scaled the highest peaks.[3] Each soul sees how much moral fortitude the person mustered to use his or her body to serve the Creator and make the world spiritually perfect. When the soul sees that its time in a body was well spent, it feels indescribable joy and unimaginable pleasure.

There is beautiful symbolism in the idea that Adam's body was made of dust from the holiest place on earth (the future location of the altar in the Jews' Temple). A holy place is where God shows His Presence in a way that we can feel close to Him. An altar is where one repents and is forgiven. Thus, Adam's creation from dust at the site of the Temple altar symbolizes that man can always draw close to the Almighty. Even if we stray very far from our spiritual missions, we can always repent and stand again in the Divine Presence.

The idea that man was composed of dust from the altar's location implies that God will never give up on us, nor should we ever give up on ourselves. We always have the potential to be the spiritually great people that our Creator intended us to become.

We should never think that we have wasted so much time, or are so entrenched in the wrong things, that it's too late to change. Better late than never! When we regret the time and opportunities that we wasted, we should resolve to do our best not to repeat our past mistakes. That can motivate us to turn our misdeeds into a powerful force that impels us to serve and love our Creator. Such misdeeds are even considered meritorious if they transport us to such a holy place.

Implications for Us

There is a Talmudic story about a great Torah scholar, Elisha ben Abuya, who became an apostate. When he turned his back on Judaism, he was nicknamed Acher, meaning "other." When his student Rabbi Meir asked him why he didn't repent, Acher said, "I heard a heavenly voice decree, 'Repent you backsliding children,[4] except for Acher.'" Acher never repented, and, as a result, his soul suffered terribly in the next world.[5]

The saddest part of the story, though, is that there was no such voice. Acher heard that everyone can repent, except for someone who is Acher—someone who stays away from God. As long as he viewed himself as Acher, he couldn't repent. If he had only seen himself as Elisha ben Abuya, he would have seen that the door to repentance and accessing God was always open.

People who live less-than-exemplary lives may rationalize that they have been doing it for so long that they can't change, or that there's no point in changing. That is the "dust" in us talking, the part that says that we're not worthwhile. Yet that same lowly dust can help us realize that living disconnected from our Creator is an empty life indeed. The Almighty loves us so much, He wants nothing more than for us to be close to Him by following His plan for how we should live. All we have to do is repent and we become holy people who invite the Divine Presence into our lives.

Notes
1. Genesis 2:7.
2. Rabbi Moshe Chaim Luzzatto discusses these concepts in *The Way of God*, I, chapters 2 and 3.
3. *Sukkah* 52a says, "Rabbi Yehudah expounded: 'In the future, the Holy One, Blessed is He, will bring the evil inclination and slaughter it in the presence of the righteous and in the presence of the wicked. To the righteous the evil inclination will appear like a high mountain that can hardly be scaled, and to the wicked it will appear like a strand of hair that can easily be snapped. These will weep and these too will weep. The righteous will weep and say, 'How were we able to overcome such a high mountain?' And the wicked will weep and say, 'How were we not able to overcome this strand of hair?'"
4. Jeremiah 3:14.
5. *Hagigah* 14b-15b.

The First People

Anthropologists say that the first people were primitive, ape-like beings. They lived hundreds of thousands of years ago in small groups in caves or in simple shelters, hunting and gathering food. They did not know how to cultivate crops, write language, or build homes. Their vocabulary was probably not more than a few hundred words. (That would have made it hard to do the *Caveman Times* crossword puzzles!) They used rudimentary tools that they found in their environment, such as wood, bone, clay, or stone. Those whom anthropologists believe lived tens of thousands of years ago sometimes decorated crude pottery, animal skins, and cave walls with pictures made from natural dyes.[1]

This early man often seems more like an animal than a civilized human. Moreover, archaeologists say that for hundreds of thousands of years, early people never developed a civilization, complex technology, or a culture based on language and transmitted stories.[2]

Archaeological finds show that, apparently out of nowhere, people in the Near East suddenly started developing sophisticated architecture, pottery, agriculture, and specialized trades around 6000 years ago. For the first time, large towns and empires, bronze tools and weapons, writing and records, and complex social, political, and religious systems appeared.[3]

Perhaps we can shed light on how and why this sudden change occurred.

The medieval Jewish commentator, Nachmanides, wrote that God created a precursor to Adam when He made the higher animals on the sixth day.[4] These could have been the early people who resembled modern man physically, but who lacked divine souls.

Adam was the first human who possessed a divine soul, as Genesis says:

> *And the Lord God formed man* [from] *dust from the earth, and He blew in his nose a soul of life, and the man became a living being.*[5]

Far from being primitive, Adam and his wife had tremendous spiritual potential, clarity, and vision. The Talmud[6] expresses this by saying that the first person, meaning Adam, could see from one end of the world to the other. In other words, he understood how everything in the material world was to be used for spiritual purposes.

Perhaps we can integrate anthropological findings with the Torah as follows: Human-like beings without divine souls could have come into being before Adam and Eve and lived in prehistoric times, while the first people who had Godly souls started new civilizations that made major changes in the way that people lived.

Implications for Us

Fossilized bones can't tell us what kind of souls or moral values their owners had. The important history of humanity is not told by fossils and mummies but rather by the spiritual contributions that people made to better humanity. Once man was created, Genesis focuses on how people are supposed to see their lives as having a spiritual purpose and how God wants people to contribute to the moral perfection of the world. Unfortunately, people often use their free will to indulge their personal desires and bring spiritual ruin instead.[7]

The true history of human beings began when the Almighty gave us His spiritual genes. Beginning our story in this way reminds us of our inherent greatness and encourages us to live up to our divine calling.

Notes

1. The Lascaux cave complex in France is famous for its paintings. Anthropologists believe it contains some of the earliest known art, which they date from 25,000 to 13,000 BCE. The paintings consist mostly of realistic images of large animals, which are known from fossils to have lived in the area at the time, as well as human handprints.
2. By definition, prehistory means before there was written language. During the Stone Age, early people were hunters and gatherers and lived in small groups. The Neolithic era, which ended the Stone Age, is when paleontologists believe the first agricultural settlements began, and with them, increased technology and more developed civilization.
3. The Early Bronze Age in the Near East is most often characterized as the first great period of urbanism in the Near East. The material culture there reflected a trend towards living in urban settlements and social organization into cities. Some scholars call this era "the Emergence of Cities." Starting around 3500 BCE, there arose complex civilizations in the river valleys, characterized by hierarchical government and administration. Writing and literate societies appeared who irrigated their crops and had large-scale public works. From "The Early Bronze Age of the Levant," on ancientneareast.net.
4. Maharal's commentary on Genesis 2:7, referring to Genesis 1:25.
5. Genesis 2:7.
6. *Hagigah* 12a.
7. Generations who lived after Adam and Eve became increasingly immoral, and their moral decline was mirrored in people's appearances. For example, the Talmud says (*Sanhedrin* 109a) that some of the people who tried to wage war against God in the story of the Tower of Babel became apes!

Why Have Commandments?

And the Lord God took the person and He placed him in the Garden of Eden, in order to work it and to guard it. And the Lord God commanded the person saying, "From every tree in the Garden you may surely eat. And from the Tree of Knowledge of Good and Evil you should not eat of it, for in the day you eat of it you shall surely die."[1]

Judaism teaches that God created people because He, being totally good, wanted recipients to whom He could give His love. Yet, were we to receive this love with no effort on our part, two disadvantages would result:

The first disadvantage is that we would feel ashamed at continually receiving handouts that we did not earn, for our greatest satisfaction comes from achieving results through hard work. By creating a spiritually imperfect world, the Almighty gave us the opportunity to find meaning and purpose as we work to perfect this world and ourselves. He continually places spiritual obstacles in our path to give us the opportunity to overcome them. If we do, He delights in rewarding us in a spiritual afterlife according to the effort that we made to do His will.

The second disadvantage is that we would not cherish our relationship with Him. God gave us human relationships so that we could learn how to relate to Him. Just as two friends' or a husband's and wife's love and appreciation for each other is commensurate with how much they sacrifice for one another, we deepen our relationship with our Creator the more we invest ourselves in doing what He asks of us.

The Lord created the Garden of Eden for the first couple with everything they needed, yet He denied them one thing—eating fruit of the Tree of Knowledge of Good and Evil. Adam and Eve's purpose was to obey their one commandment and thus make the world spiritually perfect. Had they obeyed God's command, they and their descendants would have lived in the Garden forever, having earned the reward of an eternally close bond with their Creator in Paradise. When Adam and Eve failed to obey God, it became their descendants' task to spiritually fix the world by following God's will for humanity.

What was at stake can be seen in Adam's name, as Biblical Hebrew reflects the essence of the person or object it describes. Although Adam means "taken from the earth" (*adamah*), it also relates to the words *adameh l'elyon*—"I will be like the One on High."[2]

Whatever has potential for bad has an equal potential for good.[3] For example, eating has tremendous ability to draw us close to God, provided that we appreciate that He is the One who is providing us with nourishment and the pleasure of eating. We can delight in the tastes, aromas, and colors of the food that we ingest, and say a blessing before and after we eat, acknowledging the divine source of our food. We can eat only food that is kosher, which is the only food that can be spiritually elevated. We can think while eating that we are eating to nourish our bodies so that they can do our Creator's work. These thoughts allow us to transform eating into a sublime activity that elevates the body to the level of the soul. On the other hand, if we eat non-kosher food, its spiritual potential cannot be unlocked, and so it drags down our body and soul. If we eat food that is harmful to our bodies, we disrespect the divine intention that food has for our bodies, and it cannot help our souls do their work. If we eat more food than our bodies need, or eat as an end in itself, we indulge that animalistic drive as an end in itself. That lowers our bodies and souls in the process.

Sex, which has the capacity to draw a divine soul into a body and create a human life, has even greater potential than food does for sanctification and good. That is why it has an equal and opposite potential for bad and is so often degraded and abused.

Earth, from which man was created, is neutral. By itself, it is lowly and lifeless, but it has enormous potential to nurture. A person's physical makeup is animalistic and materialistic, but the Godly soul inside gives the person the potential to grow spiritually.

The earth in us can be destructive if we let our "earthy" animalistic drives and instincts guide us. An animal has no intrinsic moral/spiritual potential to develop: Genesis terms the land animals *behaima,* from the words *ba mah,* meaning "it is already what it is." Animals can't develop in themselves higher forms of self-expression; neither can they make moral choices. Animals can only follow their instincts and are unable to be good or bad.

If we are self-centered or hedonistic, using our bodies without regard for how God wants us to use them, we block the soul's connection with the Source of all blessing and become worse than animals. We are supposed to guide the wonderful potential growth of our earthly nature by using our minds to curb our animalistic and egocentric desires and direct them in spiritually constructive ways.

We were created to make ourselves like the One Above—being just, honest, giving, moral, and rejecting of evil. Had Adam rejected evil and only obeyed his Creator, he would have earned a spiritual reward that was more pleasurable than all of the physical delights that were in the Garden of Eden. Had Adam done what God asked,[4] he would have shown that his body was one with his soul, and that both were in sync with the Creator's will. This is one suggestion as to why God gave Adam a commandment to observe as soon as he was created.

Unfortunately, Adam divorced his body from God's will for him and thereby became subject to his body's limitations. His disobedience severed the incredibly close tie that the Almighty wanted people to have with Him. When Adam removed his body from its only source of eternity, he brought mortality upon himself and his descendants. Whenever we live as if we are only physical, we inevitably die because nothing physical lasts forever. Our soul and the spiritual contributions that we make are immortal. The only way for a body to achieve immortality is for it to connect perfectly to its Source.

Adam's sin not only made it impossible for him to receive all of the blessings that God wished to give him, it made it necessary for all of humanity to take a much longer route to spiritually perfecting itself and the world. What Adam could have achieved in a day, we are still trying to accomplish 5,768 years later.

A body created from earth reminds us that we sometimes need to be passive as dirt and submit to our Creator's will for us. This is one explanation for why the name Adam consists of the Hebrew letter *alef* and the Hebrew word *dom*, meaning "silent." In the numerical system of *gematria*, where each letter in the Hebrew alphabet has a value, the letter *alef* has the value of one. Thus, "Adam" can be taken to mean "the one who is silent." Adam was supposed to accept the Almighty's plan for how to live, but it's not always easy to subjugate our personal desires to divine commands. People like to be their own bosses and chart their own courses without some authority telling them what to do. That is why the Talmud says that someone who does what the Almighty commands him to do is superior to someone who does a good deed because it feels right, it makes sense to him, or he simply wants to do it.[5] We instinctively rebel against taking orders and want to be the final arbiters of how to live. We have to work very hard to make the divine will our will. Many of us would prefer God to have given us the Ten Suggestions instead of the Ten Commandments.

Serving God on His Terms

People sometimes think that we should live by moral codes that we create. The Torah tells us that believing in God and having a relationship with Him means following His system of laws, not our own sense of right and wrong.

Why can't we define the terms by which we have a relationship with God? The Torah tells us that since time immemorial, people did what they thought was morally right. They worshiped idols, sacrificed their children to idols, stole, had inappropriate sex, or, in Adam's case, ate forbidden fruit. They all believed that their behavior would bring them closer to God. There was only one problem—God didn't agree with them!

Implications for Us

We learn from Adam's downfall that professing faith in God is not enough. We must back up beliefs by the right actions. When we only develop ideas about spirituality that make us feel close to God, it is like daydreaming about someone we love.

We can only really be close to someone whom we know and understand. Spiritually perfecting ourselves means becoming as much like our Creator as possible. We can only be like Him if we act in ways that He defines as good and desirable. How and what does He want us to give? How and to whom does He want us to be compassionate? What are His definitions of fairness and justice? How does He want us to be holy? The Torah and the Oral Law (Talmud) answer these questions. We learn about God by studying His Torah, which expresses His "thoughts," so to speak; by applying those ideas to the world around us; and by doing what the Torah tells us to do.

Any relationship can only be as strong as the less-committed partner. God always wants to have a total relationship with us. We can measure our commitment by the degree to which we accept our Partner's advice on how to make this relationship succeed. Thinking about, reading about, or developing a feeling for the One Above allows us to relate to Him only superficially. We don't begin to know God until we learn about and act like Him, thus concretizing what He stands for.

Love in Deed is Love Indeed

If one wants to learn music, psychotherapy, sports, medicine, or how to raise children, one must apply the knowledge to real life. When we actually put our intellectual knowledge into practice, we develop a totally different appreciation for what we have learned and for our teachers who are masters in their fields.

Thinking about the Almighty without acting in ways that He tells us are the foundation of a mutual relationship is like studying a topic without applying it to real life. Our knowledge stays superficial and we have only a shallow connection to our interest. We can study how to play the violin, but until we spend many hours actually practicing, we will neither become a true musician nor appreciate the greatness of master violinists. As we sacrifice our time and energy to develop our passion, our love for it becomes deeper and deeper.

In similar fashion, we become experts at having a relationship with our Creator when we spend many hours studying about, thinking about, and acting like Him. We must express our feelings and beliefs in deed because the deepest and most lasting love is built when we do loving things for someone. God continually does things for us, and we should love Him for what He gives us. Yet we will love Him more if we continually do things to show our commitment to Him.

There is a limit to how much a person can love someone for whom they do nothing. The more we do, the more we love. If no actions sustain the love, it will soon die of malnutrition. When a mother gives of herself physically and emotionally, day and night, to provide for her baby, it can result in a profound love. A woman who makes few sacrifices for her child, who hires people to take care of him from infancy until he grows up, may love her child much less.

Many marriages founder today because couples assume that love appears by magic. When it disappears, they think it cannot be resurrected. Love often disappears because partners stop doing loving acts for each other. If they resume doing the things that made them love each other in the first place, the marriage can thrive again.

The same applies to our relationship with God. God constantly provides us with nourishment, a place to live, clothing, and functioning bodies, as well as many kinds of pleasures. If we want to truly love God, we must show our commitment to our relationship by responding behaviorally on His terms.

This is why the Hebrew word for commandment, *mitzvah*, has the word *tzav* at its root. *Tzav* means "attachment." God's intention in giving us commandments is to provide us with ongoing opportunities to attach our souls to Him. If we value that intimacy, we will do whatever He asks of us. When we keep ourselves at arm's length, we avoid committing ourselves to the relationship.

Many modern people expect pleasures and rewards to come easily, without effort and struggle. We can learn from God's command to Adam that nothing truly worthwhile comes without effort. If we try our best to live according to His will, even when it doesn't make sense to us, our efforts will always bear fruit.

Notes

1. Genesis 2:15-16.
2. *Zohar Chadash* 2:178.
3. This kabbalistic concept is known as "*zeh l'umat zeh.*"
4. Adam's single command encompassed six of the Seven Noahide laws that all humanity was later supposed to keep. The Noahide laws encompass about 70 of the 613 commandments in the Torah. Jews can only observe about one-third of these 613 today because many commandments are applicable only when there is a Jewish Temple in Jerusalem, and/or the majority of Jews live in Israel.
5. *Bava Kamma* 87a.

Part II:
The Garden of Eden

Eating in the Garden of Eden

The Garden of Eden story that many of us learned as children cannot be understood at face value. By carefully analyzing the original text, we will find it to be rich with meaning:

> *And the Lord God planted a garden in Eden* [Aden] *from the east* [mikedem] *and He placed there the man that He had formed. And the Lord God caused to sprout from the ground every tree that is pleasant to look at and good to eat, as well as the Tree of Life in the middle of the garden, and the Tree of Knowledge of Good and Evil.[1]*
>
> *The Lord God took the man and put him in the Garden of Eden to work it and guard it. And the Lord God commanded the man saying, "You may surely eat from every tree in the Garden, and from the Tree of Knowledge of Good and Evil you must not eat from it, because in the day you eat of it you will certainly die."[2]*

Garden of Divine Purpose . . .

The word *aden* means "refined." Something that is coarse or unrefined has a layer that covers its higher, or better, purpose. The Garden of Eden was so named because the spiritual purpose of every tree, plant, and animal was apparent. One didn't have to search deeper than what one saw to see that everything there had no purpose other than to serve its Creator. Adam was able to see the spiritual purpose of everything to such an extent that when the Creator brought all of the animals to him,[3] he gave them Hebrew names that expressed each species' spiritual essence and its unique role in a divinely orchestrated world.

The Creator put the first people in this Paradise, where divine purpose shone everywhere, so that they would use it all to draw close to Him. The sight, aroma, and taste of each permitted fruit was a gift from—and connection to—the Creator. Had Adam used these fruits only as the Almighty designed them to be used, he would have spiritually perfected the world. Instead, he used his free will to serve his own purposes.

. . . in a World that Hides God

The Hebrew word for "world," *olam*, comes from the root *he'elem*, meaning "hidden." God designed the world so that it would hide Him, yet people could still find Him in the complexities of nature and the goings-on of daily life. Our free will allows us to look at a waterfall, a flower, or a baby and say, "Isn't that beautiful?" or "Isn't nature amazing?" without connecting to the One who put everything here. If we think instead, "How wonderful God is for giving us such beauty!" or "How amazing is the Creator for making such complex and incredible creations! Let's thank Him for it," we reveal His Presence and use the world as He intended.

Joy and Trust

Eating is central to many Jewish rituals. We celebrate holidays, the Sabbath, and lifecycle events with meals. Food is such a basic form of connecting to people that the Almighty made it the primary way that a baby connects to its mother. As we mature, we can sanctify our primal drive for nourishment by abstaining from foods that cannot be spiritually elevated (i.e., foods that are not kosher) and by eating permitted foods only after offering blessings acknowledging their divine source. If we were to take in our nourishment aware of—and in accordance with the wishes of—the loving Being who constantly provides for us, eating would be a joyous act of continually deepening our love for God and our sense of being loved.

If, instead, we only relate to food as an end in itself, we form a relationship with our appetite and the momentary pleasures that the physical world offers.

God wanted to teach the first couple to trust that He will give people exactly what we need if we follow His rules. We may not be able to comprehend how He will do that, but the more we trust, the more we see how He continually takes care of us because He loves us more than we can fathom.

Implications for Us

One obstacle to our living in trust and connection to the Almighty is our desire for independence. Adam disobeyed his Creator because he wanted to be independent. People often want to decide for themselves how to live. We want to express our individuality, to do our "own thing," to be self-made men and women. We want to live unencumbered by rules and be free to do whatever we want.

Adam and Eve were challenged not to eat a forbidden fruit, and they failed to rise to the challenge. By trusting our Creator to know what is best for us, and by rejecting the "forbidden fruits" that confront us every day, we can bring the world back to Paradise.

Notes
1. Genesis 2:8-9.
2. Genesis 2:16-17.
3. See Genesis 2:19-20.

Knowledge that Stunts Growth

Losing Objectivity

Contrary to popular belief, we are not necessarily better off knowing all there is to know. We tend to think knowledge is totally good and will make us independent and powerful. We sometimes think that the more we know, the less we have to obey an outside moral force because we have the tools to make our own decisions.

That only the Tree of Knowledge of Good and Evil was off limits to Adam suggests that some types of knowledge are not good and can't be used constructively. Some types of knowledge are not good for us because they consist of an intimate knowledge of evil that corrupts the mind and harms the body. God forbade Adam to ingest a fruit that confuses people as to what is truly good or bad.

When Adam was created, he only had an abstract idea as to what sin and evil were. As long as he stayed naive, he could be totally objective about what was good and what was evil, what was true and what was false.

God wanted Adam to have a superficial knowledge of evil—just enough to avoid it. Once Adam ate of the forbidden fruit,[1] he internalized knowledge of evil. Evil now resided inside of Adam, actually becoming a part of him. This would forever taint his clarity about what is right and wrong.

We can understand the symbolism behind the Tree of Knowledge better by considering that fruit is to the body what knowledge is to the soul. We internalize both fruit and knowledge and they become part of us. Just as we should not poison our bodies with junk food that looks appealing or tastes good, we should not poison our minds and souls with tantalizing information that stunts our spiritual development.

Experiencing Unwholesome Pleasures and Temptations

The story of the Tree of Knowledge of Good and Evil highlights the insight that it is much easier to avoid something whose physical pleasures we haven't experienced and whose effects we don't crave than it is to reject something that we know first-hand is exquisitely gratifying. Eating the forbidden fruit gave humanity a strong desire to want to do more wrong things. Before eating the forbidden fruit, Adam was like someone who had never smoked tobacco or used cocaine. Such a person may hear that these substances exist but won't crave them. Once he tries them and discovers how pleasurable they are, he is strongly drawn to indulge more, for having read that these substances are poison is no match for the immediate pleasure they offer. He discounts the dire warnings of future consequences as he happily gets pleasure now.

So it is for us. Once we experience spiritually unwholesome pleasures, it takes far more conviction and self-discipline to reject them than it took to ignore them in the first place. This concept is expressed in the Talmudic saying, "In the [elevated] place that a penitent stands, a wholly righteous person cannot stand."[2]

Blurring Lines Between Good and Evil

Eating the forbidden fruit made evil and falsehood part of Adam and Eve and their descendants (to whom they passed their spiritual "genes" and shortcomings). It is very hard for us to sense how spiritually destructive some actions can be, because the effect of the forbidden fruit was to blur the lines between right and wrong. Since then, people rarely objectively evaluate what is spiritually best. In today's world, we see this when modern Westerners are unwilling to say that anything is categorically bad. Many of them say, "You have your truth and others have their truth. I can't judge what is right and what is wrong." Even acts such as Nazi genocide of the Jews during the Holocaust or current terrorism against Jews are not universally condemned. This is but one example of how blurred the distinction between right and wrong are, even today.

Implications for Us

People who live in a democracy value having a free press, yet a free press is a double-edged sword. Allowing people to print whatever they please can educate people about subjects that are useful or important to know, yet it can also cause great damage. Once we have been exposed to certain information, it affects us, and we can't "unknow" what we hear and see. A free press can be used to defame people, spread lies, and publicize biased information. It can harm people by overexposing them to violence, sex, and bad values. Publicizing how to exploit people or make bombs and exposing covert rescue missions has even led to people losing their lives.

As we are bombarded by information via television, radio, books, newspapers, magazines, movies, and computers, we need to be able to distinguish which of that information is constructive, which is neutral, and which is destructive.

We should be discriminating in what we allow ourselves and our children to see and hear, avoiding exposure to spiritually damaging ideas, graphics, and media. Frequent exposure to stories and pictures depicting violence, sex, alcohol and drug use, self-centeredness, disrespect to parents and teachers, and the like dulls our spiritual sensitivities. Once we ingest these "fruits" into our psyches, it is very hard to rid ourselves of their negative influence.

The average American child sees more than 100,000 acts of violence and more than 10,000 murders on television by the time that he or she is 18. In 2001, about 85% of television sitcoms, movies, and soap operas contained sexual images or references. Movies almost invariably expose us to even more sex and violence. Pornographic sites are among the most popular on the Internet. Immersing ourselves in so much sex and violence necessarily degrades how we relate to others.

Imagine what would happen if, instead, each child saw 100,000 acts of kindness or 10,000 programs showing respectful and moral behavior during his or her most impressionable years! If we are not willing to limit our—and our children's—exposure to negativity, we should at least try to counterbalance it by doing a comparably impressive number of acts of charity, kindness, and moral self-restraint.

Notes
1. Genesis 3:7.
2. *Berachot* 34b.

Men and Women

It became popular during the 1970s to view men and women as basically the same. The pendulum swung the other way in the early 1990s with books such as John Gray's *Men are from Mars, Women are from Venus*. Let's see what Genesis and Judaism have to say about the nature of the first couple:

> *In the image of God He created him* [Adam]. *Male and female He created them.*[1]

While most Biblical translations refer to Adam as a male, the Talmud understood Adam to be a Siamese twin whom God later separated into two separate people.[2] This is based on the above verse, which first calls Adam "*him*," then says "male and female He created *them*." According to this way of reading the verse, the first person was initially one being who was male *and* female.[3]

While many books and scientific articles insist that men and women are very different, the reasons *why* both sexes exist are rarely addressed. Genesis and the Talmud enlighten us about this:

> *The Lord God said, "It is not good, a person's being alone. I will make for the person a helper against himself." And the Lord God had formed from the earth all of the animals of the field and every fowl in the heavens. And He brought them to Adam to see what he would call each. And whatever Adam called each living being, that is its name. And Adam gave names to every animal, and to every bird of the heavens, and to every animal of the field. And Adam found no helper against himself.*[4]

Group Purpose vs. Individual Purpose

Adam gave Hebrew names to each animal species, while he, his wife, and their descendants each got individual names. The animals didn't get individual names because objects and animals only have purposes as collective groups. Each human being has a name because each has an individual purpose.

God had Adam name the animals before he received his wife so that Adam would understand that no animal could possibly be a proper partner for him. He needed a soul mate with whom he would share intimacy and caring, who would be his equal intellectually, emotionally, and spiritually. Only after Adam yearned for, and presumably expressed his need for, such a relationship[5] did the Almighty create woman as a separate entity.

Same Species, Unique Gifts

The fact that God eventually separated the man and the woman into two separate entities tells us that they were not meant to be identical or accomplish the same goals. God deliberately made men and women different so that each would contribute his or her unique gifts to each other and to the world. More than 3,300 years ago, the Torah expressed the view that "men are from Mars" and "women are from Venus." By living together harmoniously on Earth, each can help the other to grow spiritually beyond their starting points.

A truly intimate marriage requires two partners who are not identical to one another and who can give what the other lacks. Men have also typically brought things from the world to their wives, and their wives have refined these things into something better that benefits the entire family. For example, men brought things such as meat, flax, animal skins, and money.[6] The wives then refined them into usable items such as food, clothing, and necessities for the home or for living.

The story of woman's creation tells us that God made woman man's equal partner. The first woman had the man's same potential spiritual greatness, yet she could be more objective about his character strengths and weaknesses and lovingly motivate him to change so that he would achieve his potential.[7] This type of constructive criticism often creates tension, yet a spiritually attuned man will welcome it and respond positively, seeing his wife as his helper. A man who wants complacency instead of growth will feel only his wife's opposition, or a "helper against him." The Torah and

Jewish prayers term God a helper, reinforcing the concept that women imitate the Almighty by helping people grow.[8]

Adam understood that "an oppositional partner" would cause him tension. Yet he knew that he would stagnate if left alone. Still, God did not make Adam a partner who would cause him discomfort until he expressed his desire for such a mate.

Implications for Us

Today, many singles remain so because they don't want to compromise their "freedom," yet their singlehood comes at a spiritual and emotional cost. The Midrash says that a man who has no wife lives without good, without help, without joy, without blessing, without atonement, without peace, without life, and is incomplete.[9] A greater fulfillment comes with the continual giving and self-improvement in marriage than can be achieved by being single. It behooves singles who have fears of intimacy or marriage to work out those feelings so that they can avail themselves of the growth and fulfillment of being a spouse.

Gender Equality

Men and women's differences are supposed to help both grow. In most societies today, success and power are still largely defined in male terms (physical prowess, visibility, having money and possessions, competing), not female ones (creating, nurturing, collaborating). Judaism teaches that men and women, with their respective qualities, are equally important in making the world what it should be.

Although we often refer to God as He, God has neither gender nor body. He has both "male" (kabbalistically described as acting on, and being a Giver to the world) and "female" (kabbalistically described as receiving and nurturing) attributes. Everyone has opportunities to imitate the divine by exercising both of these aspects in daily life.

Takers into Givers

The Torah commands men,[10] but not women,[11] to marry and have children. The Torah only commands us to do things that we might not do of our own accord. Men, more than women, often find it difficult to make the attitude changes that require going from being takers to givers, and from wanting independence to wanting interdependence in marriage.[12]

God made men and women with enormous differences that require human skills and divine help to bridge. This means learning what those differences are and how to bridge them, and sometimes getting professional help or advice from those more knowledgeable than we are about how to have harmonious relationships. At the same time, we need to pray for divine guidance in choosing and in being an appropriate marriage partner if we want to be happily married.

Growth vs. Comfort

We often think that the purpose of life is to be as comfortable as possible and that something is wrong when life is difficult. We take medications to deal with aches and medical problems instead of eating properly, exercising, changing our lives to have less stress, and so on. Alcohol and drugs offer easy ways to escape discomfort.

Close to half of all American marriages end in divorce. When the relationship becomes uncomfortable for any number of reasons, few spouses fix themselves and develop the tools to deal with the problems in the marriage. Instead, they often dispose of the marriage and try to find an easier situation with less conflict. (Unfortunately, this fails too because second marriages typically fare worse than first ones![13])

Genesis tells us that some kinds of discomfort present opportunities for growth. By appreciating and valuing what others have to offer, including their constructive criticism, we can better ourselves. Growing from, instead of avoiding, these challenges can help us make the most of our lives.

Notes

1. Genesis 1:27.
2. *Brachot* 61a. See also Zohar *Shemot* 55a.
3. Rather than refer to Adam as s/he prior to the time of separation into Adam and Eve, it is easier to refer to Adam as "him." God communicated separately with Adam and Eve when they were still one entity that looked like Siamese twins.
4. Genesis 2:19-20.
5. Nachmanides on Genesis 2:20.
6. *Yevamot* 63a.
7. Contemporary women often marry men hoping the men will change. This is a bad idea because most men will not want to change in the ways that the woman wants. The woman's desire to motivate her husband to change only finds a healthy place in marriage if the husband's vision of himself or his marriage includes changing in the ways that the wife wants!
8. Among other ways, men imitate the Almighty by studying Torah and incorporating its ideas into their behavior and interactions with the material world and those they encounter in the public realm. This requires being honest in business, creating a just legal system, and disbursing charity. While women can do much of this, they tend to contribute more than men in the realm of personal relationships.
9. *Genesis Rabbah* 17.
10. In Genesis 1:8, God commands Adam to be fruitful and multiply, and this is reiterated in Genesis 9:7. Jewish men are commanded to marry and try to have at least one male and one female child. (*Yevamot* 6:6)
11. Tosefta on *Yevamot* 8:2. The structure of marriage requires men to be givers to their wives. The Torah requires men to support their wives financially and to fulfill the wives' needs for intimacy. The *Mishnah Torah, Hilchot Ishut*, chapters 12-14, details some of the man's obligations to become a giver to his wife and children.
12. Although statistics fluctuate from study to study, 50% of first marriages, 67% of second, and 74% of third marriages in the United States end in divorce, according to Jennifer Baker of the Forest Institute of Professional Psychology in Springfield, Missouri. Quoted on Divorcerate.org, January 2007.

Eve's Creation

Once Genesis indicates why woman was necessary in God's plan for the world (Adam needed a partner who could help him bring the world to spiritual perfection), it explains how she was created:

> *And the Lord God caused a deep sleep to fall on Adam and he slept. And God took one of the ribs and closed the flesh underneath. And the Lord God built [vayiven] the rib which He had taken from the man into a woman and He brought her to the man.[1]*

The Talmudic Sages debated whether Adam and Eve were initially joined face-to-face or back-to-back before God separated them. The rabbis decided that the couple was back-to-back. This "Talmudic hair-splitting" was their way of raising the question of whether men and women have separate personas ("back to back") or merely superficial differences (seeing "eye-to-eye"). The Sages concluded that men and women have different personas.[2]

By separating Adam into a woman and a man, God created two people who could each give to the other what he or she lacked individually. As such, they could create something that was greater than the sum of their parts, including children.

Jewish tradition suggests that men generally express their spirituality by ridding the world of negativity. For example, men may try to destroy evil by fighting wars or bad people, uprooting injustice, and so on. Women tend to express their spirituality by nurturing and taking care of others. In other words, men's desire to rid the world of negativity is paralleled by women's desire to nurture and contribute the positive.

God does both. He exercises overt power, which tends to be seen as a masculine trait. He also nurtures, which is often viewed as a feminine trait. The Almighty wanted men and women to develop their respective attributes of power/control and nurturing in healthy ways.

The Truly Powerful Man

For example, before or in addition to ridding the world of evil, men need to subdue their own negative inclinations. "Who is a powerful person? One who conquers his negative inclination. As it is said, 'He who is slow to anger is better than the strong man, and one who rules his passions is better than the conqueror of a city.'"[3]

If a man first works on becoming a humble person who puts God in the center of his life, he will not center his life around seeking power, excessive admiration, and personal gain. His opinions and behavior will not be molded by the promises and gifts of those who can give him money and prestige. He will not lose his moral compass as he works to eliminate poverty, disease, ignorance, violence, crime, social injustice, and the like.

Rather, he will ask how God wants the world to look, based on the divine will expressed in the Torah, and how he should behave in it. He will destroy evil by teaching others how to live in a Godly way and demonstrating that way of living himself.

When a man relates to others, he should see their divine image and not exploit them to serve his physical or psychological desires. He can help rid the world of evil by making sure that he doesn't use people, by controlling his temper, and by treating others with respect instead of trying to control them.

Men can discipline their children as a way of educating them and helping them grow as responsible individuals instead of reacting with anger or disapproval because they didn't fulfill the parents' expectations.

The Truly Powerful Woman

Women can make sure they never fall into the trap of acting undignified when they seek and give love. Women nurture best when their self-esteem doesn't depend on others' responses to them. If a woman puts the Almighty and His will for her in the center of her life, she will not degrade herself in order to love and be loved. If she sees the divine image in herself, she will find and nurture fulfilling, healthy relationships.

When people are desperate, or don't have good self-esteem, they often give for the wrong reasons, such as to get something in return, or without considering the negative long-term results of overdoing it. Such unbridled giving by parents can create spoiled children or foster irresponsibility or dependency in adults.

The Powerful Couple

When a couple has healthy aspects of both power and nurturing, they can bring the divine Presence into their lives instead of having power struggles and discord. A healthy balance occurs when a husband helps his wife set limits and she helps him become more emotionally vulnerable and giving. The foundation of a Jewish marriage is based on a man's providing for his wife's practical, emotional, and sexual needs, which gives him concrete opportunities to conquer his tendency toward egocentricity. Simultaneously, this type of marriage gives women a grounded framework within which they can continually give and nurture.

Before God brought the first woman to Adam, the Talmud says that He "braided Eve's hair."[4] To this day, brides commonly have their hair "done up" to make themselves beautiful on their wedding day. The Talmud mentions this to let us know that God made women beautiful so that men would be attracted to them. The physical attraction between men and women is meant to open the door for a relationship, but not be its main foundation. The foundation should be built from giving to each other in ways that develop spiritual and emotional bonds. This involves attentive listening, empathic communication, giving emotional and practical support, creating intimacy, and helping each other achieve his or her potential.

Genesis uses a very strange word for woman's creation. It says that she was "built" (*vayiven*) from Adam's rib.[5] The Hebrew word *vayiven* is related to the word *binah*, meaning "understanding." The Talmud explains that God gave women more understanding of people than men typically have, while men are often endowed with greater analytical reasoning.[6] The words *binah* and *vayiven* come from the same Hebrew root meaning "within." We build by taking something, such as a stack of lumber or a mound of bricks, and expanding it outwards. Seeing a three-story building, one can conceptualize how the parts need to come together in order to end up with the larger whole. Similarly, we often comprehend people by gaining an understanding of how they are put together.

Implications for Us

Every aspect of the way we were created is supposed to teach us spiritual messages. Men and women as a whole were created with different faculties so that together they could make the world spiritually perfect. (Of course, there are some men who have more "female" qualities and some women who have more "male" qualities. That is fine. Sometimes such people even marry each other and have wonderful marriages!) It is pointless to argue about which sex is better or to try to do away with our differences. By focusing on what we can each contribute to the betterment of the world, we can spiritually improve ourselves and those around us.

Notes
1. Genesis 2:21-22.
2. *Eruvin* 18a.
3. *Ethics of the Fathers* 4:1.
4. *Brachot* 61a.
5. Genesis 2:22.
6. *Niddah* 45b.

Joining Forces

After relating the creation of the first woman, the Torah teaches how couples with Godly souls are meant to view one another.

When Adam saw Eve, he exclaimed,

> *This time it is bone of my bones and flesh of my flesh. This [one] shall be called woman* [ishah] *because she was taken from man* [ish].[1]

What a wonderful way God designed for Adam to love his wife as himself![2] He made them both from the same body and soul.

We tend to identify most closely with, and care most about, that which we consider "ourselves." So many marital and social problems result from seeing ourselves as separate from others. If we could only see our basic similarities, we would know how hurting another person truly damages ourselves.

We can learn more about this idea by examining the Hebrew words for "man" and "woman," for these words combine to form both "fire" and "God." The words *ish* (man) and *ishah* (woman) share two Hebrew letters (*aleph* and *shin*) that spell *aish* (fire). Fire has tremendous power. When that power is harnessed constructively, fire can be used to turn metals into tools, utensils, building materials, vehicles, and so on. But when fire is unbridled, it can burn indiscriminately and destroy everything in its path.

Ish also contains the letter *yud,* while *ishah* contains the letter *heh.* These two letters, *yud* and *heh*, spell God's Hebrew name. When a man and his wife have a sense of harmony and holiness and act as one unit, they can draw the Divine Presence (symbolized by God's Name) into their union. If they ignore or misuse their inner divinity, they remove the *yud* and *heh.* Then, only the *aleph* and *shin*—fire—remain. This suggests that two people who don't know how to channel their inner fires for a higher, spiritual purpose are at risk of destroying themselves and their marriage.

Implications for Us

We fulfill our highest calling when we use our inner fires to draw the Divine Presence into our homes and into the world. Unfortunately, Jews have often used this inner fire to try to fix the world without regard for what God wants. Thus, most of the prominent 20th-century movements that were intended to change and improve the world were started, or were heavily supported, by Jews. Communism, socialism, liberalism, radical feminism, and the like are all examples. Jews who pioneered these movements felt their inner fires burning and sincerely wanted to make a better world. But trying to fix the world without putting God in the picture often creates havoc, ruin, and moral decay in the long run. Some of these movements resulted in the deaths of tens of millions of people as well as untold suffering. When we try to fix the world without considering its Creator's goals, we see how the road to hell can be paved with good intentions.

Notes

1. Genesis 2:23.
2. It has been suggested that the first woman was taken from the area under Adam's rib, which is next to the heart, so that he would love her.

Marriage and Intimacy

Once man and woman became separate entities, they formed the prototype for all marriages that would ever exist. Yet they didn't innately know how to have a successful partnership. So God gave Adam and Eve a bit of premarital advice to insure the viability of their union:

> *Therefore, a man should leave his father and his mother and cleave unto his wife and they shall be one flesh.*[1]

If Adam had no human parents, whom was he supposed to leave?! The answer is that he had to leave a mindset that all children would henceforth have. Some of his descendants would have to literally leave their parents to have a successful marriage, while all would have to leave behind the child's dependency on those who raised them.

Mindsets: From Taking to Giving

Parents tend to give, and children tend to take, as long as the children are unmarried. Singles need to abandon their self-centered expectations if they want to have a good marriage. The above verse means that an ideal husband and father is one who primarily sees himself as a contributor to his wife and children and who feels fulfilled by giving.

The Torah is saying that a man first leaves his parents and his "taking" role, then becomes bound to his wife by giving to her. Finally, he and his wife become one flesh. This suggests that a couple should be emotionally and spiritually bonded before completing their closeness with sexual relations. Rashi interprets "becoming one flesh" to mean that their unity culminates in both of them physically creating a child, which allows them to create and give in the greatest possible ways.

Many of the world's religions consider the body to be the soul's enemy. They view sex as a concession to the flesh and the antithesis of holiness. In some cases, sex is only considered legitimate for purposes of procreation. People from these religions who wish to be truly holy are supposed to be celibate. By contrast, the Torah maintains that a man cannot fulfill himself spiritually if he *is* celibate. Only through the most physical of acts, where the man is married and is a committed giver physically and emotionally, can a couple know the depths of pleasure and bonding that can lead to desiring the pleasure of spiritual intimacy with the Almighty. That is an overriding spiritual purpose of sex.

The great physical and emotional pleasures of sex were meant to give us an idea of just how pleasurable it can be to feel the depths of the Almighty's love for us and how deeply we can love Him. Judaism is a very practical religion. We can't yearn for something that is totally abstract. By tasting the intense love and intimacy in a marriage, we can want something equally intense in our eternal relationship with our Creator. Part of that intimacy is based on doing things for our partners and putting their needs first. Similarly, the more we sacrifice to make the Lord's will our will, the more we will feel bound to Him.

Transferring Love of Parents to Love of Spouse

Another explanation of the above verse is that we can only bond with a spouse when we channel the strong love that we felt for our parents to our marriage partner. Nachmanides understood the above verse to mean that a man will wed a woman who was once a stranger and will then be closer to her than he was with his parents. What a miraculous gift that two total strangers can create such strong love for one another!

Spiritual-Physical Intimacy

The secular world often views the sex drive as an animalistic instinct that needs to be gratified. Judaism teaches that the purpose of sex is to allow a couple to be Godlike as givers and as creators. Like all physical drives, sex is supposed to fulfill a spiritual purpose. Since the first man and woman once shared a body and soul, all of their descendants have an innate desire to unite with their soul mates to recreate that original closeness. The emotional and sexual feelings that we have for a partner were designed to motivate us to bring two "halves" of one soul together in physical union. When a couple expresses their love in a sanctified way,[2] the Divine Presence is drawn into their relationship.

Focus

The purpose of sex is spiritual elevation, not self-gratification. Spiritual elevation requires a husband and wife to be totally committed to, and focused only on, each other. The degree to which sex is made holy and intimate actually affects the quality of the soul drawn down from spiritual realms into this physical world at the time a child is created. There is an idea that the father's thoughts during sexual relations also influence the quality of the soul that God puts in the child at conception.[3] It follows that having physical relations while fantasizing about others, while drunk, or when under the influence of mind-distorting drugs is the antithesis of what sexual intimacy was meant to be. Using another person for self-gratification cannot express one's divine image nor bring one closer to his or her partner or to the Creator.

Desire for Intimacy with God

Jewish adulthood begins at puberty, rather than when someone is intellectually mature. In the United States, one can first vote at 18, drive a car starting at 16 or 18, and start drinking alcohol between 18 and 21. Jews are considered to be adults at a much earlier age and are required to observe the Torah's commandments. That is because sexual, not intellectual, maturity, with its yearning to unite with the opposite sex, is a precondition for experiencing the deepest desire for a relationship with God. Life is about always wanting to be close to Him. Once we yearn for emotional, spiritual, and physical intimacy with a partner, we can (and should) yearn for that same closeness with our Creator. The physical pleasure inherent in sex within marriage should also bring a couple closer to the Giver of that pleasure.

Sex is one of God's many ways of giving us as much pleasure as possible. The more we find intimacy with a spouse, the more the stage is set for our being able to have an intimate relationship with Him as well.

Notes
1. Genesis 2:24.
2. Sanctified means that a Jewish couple follows the laws that govern holiness in sexual relations. They must be married according to Jewish law, the woman must have properly immersed herself in a ritual bath and be permitted to be intimate with her husband, and each spouse should be focused on the other in a loving way.
3. The Alter Rebbe, an early Lubavitch Chassidic leader, discussed this. Once conception occurs, the mother's love and physical nurturing sustain the baby's growth.

The Purpose of Paradise

So far in the Creation account, man and woman exist, but have no purpose to their existence. The Torah now tells us that people need purpose and meaning:

> *And the Lord God took the man and He placed him in the Garden of Eden in order to work it and to guard it. And the Lord God commanded the man saying, "From every tree in the Garden you may certainly eat, and from the Tree of Knowledge of Good and Evil you should not eat from it, because in the day you eat of it you will certainly die."*[1]

If God is all-powerful and could make it rain at will, why did He need Adam to "work" and "guard" the Garden of Eden? Certainly a divine Gardener would do a better job than a human being would!

The Almighty didn't need man to do physical work. He asked man to tend to His Garden physically and spiritually so that Adam would feel useful and important. Our Creator wanted Adam to feel he contributed something essential to the world. He wanted Adam to feel great about being God's partner in perfecting the world and to be richly rewarded for successfully overcoming his moral challenge of refraining from eating the forbidden fruit.

What work was Adam supposed to do? According to one opinion,[2] he was to pray so that God would make it rain and vegetation would grow. The fact that Adam's relating to his Creator was an integral part of the Garden's vibrancy expresses the idea that a physical paradise is meaningless if people don't connect it to a relationship with their Creator.

Rashi thought that the service God wanted was Adam's obedience to His commands.[3] This is derived from the fact that "working" (*l'avdah*) the Garden is the same word as "service to God" (*avodah*). The word "to guard" (*l'shamrah*) also means "being careful not to transgress" (*lishmor*) God's prohibitions. Thus, Rashi explained that

Adam was no groundskeeper. The Lord placed him in the Garden of Eden so that he would have an opportunity to serve God by obeying Him. Adam would need to trust that limiting himself by God's command would be to his benefit.

Implications for Us

God told Adam exactly what he needed to do in order to have a wonderful life. Adam was supposed to be totally dependent on his Creator. Had Adam obeyed God, he would have shown that following the Almighty's command was better than learning and experiencing what felt right to him. That would have spiritually perfected the world.

We, like Adam and Eve, are also challenged to believe that divine commands are truly for our benefit. Trusting God enough to do what He wants, instead of following our ideas of what is best, has been humanity's challenge ever since and a test that we have yet to overcome.

Notes
1. Genesis 2:16-18.
2. Rashi on Genesis 2:5. Targum Yonatan says that he was supposed to obey both God's positive and negative commandments.
3. Rashi on 2:5.

Quick Fix vs. Transcendent Solution

Our negative inclination usually wants us to solve problems using a quick fix, while our Godly soul wants to find transcendent ways to fix what is wrong. God designed us to have this struggle so that we could earn reward by overcoming our self-centeredness and making our Creator and His will the focus of our lives.

The next verses tell us the process by which the first couple confronted a problem and decided to "solve" it using their own logic, which they deemed better than God's recommendations. The results were disastrous. We will soon learn how this process still applies to us.

Once the first couple was commanded not to eat of the fruit of the Tree of Knowledge of Good and Evil, God challenged their conviction via His agent of temptation—the serpent:

> *And the serpent was more cunning than all of the animals of the field which the Lord God had made. And he said to the woman, "Did God really tell you not to eat from every tree of the Garden?"[1]*

The purpose of the universe is to give humanity an arena within which we can earn divine reward for our hard work in serving our Creator. If God only commanded us to do things that we liked to do, or if we wanted to do only His will, we could not earn reward. So, the Almighty continually challenges us to test our resolve to live the way that He has told us is best.

The serpent's job was to try to convince Adam and Eve to violate God's will so they could exercise their free will to overcome that challenge. Had they obeyed Him, they would have spiritually perfected the world by showing that everything is part of a divine plan to be used to serve its Designer. The couple would have become immortal, and we would all be living in Paradise today.

The serpent began his day's work by making an overture to the woman—who by nature was more empathic and therefore more gullible than the man—calling into question whether God really had her best interests in mind. That is why the serpent is termed *nachash*, derived from the Hebrew word *l'nachesh*, "to guess." His job was to make people doubt whether God truly wanted them to do what He said was best. By making the woman believe that her Creator really didn't have her best interests in mind, he could easily convince her not to follow His command and instead follow her own logic or desires. Instead of earning eternal reward, such behavior leads to momentary pleasure at the expense of one's soul.

Every person has an inner *nachash*. Freud secularized this basic concept and termed it the "id."[2] Jewish tradition calls it the "negative inclination." It encourages us to indulge in immediate emotional or physical gratification at the expense of our souls. Without it, and without the effort to continually overcome it, we couldn't earn the extraordinary pleasure of intense, eternal intimacy with our Creator.

Serpent vs. Messiah

The numerical value of the Hebrew letters in the word *nachash* is the same as those in the word *mashiach*,[3] which means "messiah," or "anointed one." The equivalent gematrias of *nachash* and *mashiach* tell us that the serpent in the Garden of Eden and the id in us are identical forces. They are both here to help us serve God. If we overcome them, we will bring the Messiah. That is because we can only fulfill the world's spiritual purpose if we use our free will to confront something (potentially) negative and use it to do God's will.[4] The spiritual challenges that we face day by day are not accidental. Our Creator constantly watches over each of us and sends us challenges that continually test our resolve to live according to His plan for us. If something is obviously good, we achieve nothing by embracing it. If a moral challenge makes us struggle, and then we make the choice that God wants us to make, we rectify our spiritual flaws and bring greater spiritual perfection to the world.

The serpent's job in the Garden of Eden was to make Eve feel that she lacked something, and then encourage her to fix it the wrong way. That would cause her to misuse her opportunities for spiritual growth and instead disconnect her, and then Adam, from God.

Eve should have ignored the serpent's questions and realized that God's sole purpose in limiting us is for our benefit. Had she done that, she would have reinforced His role as the Master and Director of the world. She would also have shown that all temptations come from Him and that disobeying Him never benefits us in the long run.

Implications for Us

God makes us overly attracted to some pleasures, such as eating, drinking, and having sex, so that we will be sure to survive and build the world.[5] However, people often confuse the intensity of their desires and drives with the validity of indulging them as they please.

We were not created to instinctively give in to our drives and feelings, nor to be robots that have no choice but to do what is right. God gave us pleasure-seeking drives so that we would use them to spiritually elevate objects, places, ourselves, and time by connecting to the divine purpose in each. Everything has divine sparks within. It is our job to release these sparks by using the world as God tells us we should.

For example, if we eat only because we are hungry or like the taste of food, or if we have physical relationships only because they feel good, we have chained ourselves to our animalistic appetites and to the physical world. If, instead, our hunger motivates us to say a blessing before and after we eat, and we eat only kosher food, we are elevating the act of eating to one of divine service.

Similarly, if we refrain from having physical relationships outside of marriage, and have physical intimacy only within the framework set by the Torah, we can bring the Almighty into our bedrooms and sanctify even the most physical of acts.

If we talk to a friend in a way that doesn't trivialize our power of speech, and refrain from gossiping, we have just made holy our ability to speak. We do the same every time that we pray or discuss Torah ideas.

When we use technology to make the world a more moral place, to learn and teach more Torah, to instruct others about how to live better, and to combat social problems, we can transform it to something holy. When we make our homes places where we offer hospitality, teach ethical and moral behavior to our family, hold Judaism classes, and the like, we make our homes into places where the Divine Presence dwells.

The fact that something feels good tells us nothing about whether God wants us to get involved with it. A "gut reaction" may gauge how we feel emotionally but gives us no information about how something will affect our soul or the spiritual world.

Sometimes our job is to reject pleasures because they will cause spiritual damage. We shouldn't figure out how we can have a relationship with that gorgeous, sexy, married co-worker. We shouldn't lie on the insurance forms to get reimbursed for damage to our belongings that didn't occur or to claim medical reimbursement for problems that don't exist. We can't share that juicy gossip with our best friend because the Torah forbids gossiping and tale bearing. We can't yell at our parents to get angry feelings off our chest because we are required to honor those who gave us life.

The only way that we can truly know what is good or bad is by finding out what our Creator has to say about it. We learn this by studying Judaism and by asking an observant rabbi what to do when we don't know. Things that we find pleasurable in the short term are often destructive in the long run. Meanwhile, exercising self-discipline often feels terrible in the

> short run but great in the long run. Our vision is too limited to know the truly long-term effects of our actions.
>
> Some of our finest accomplishments occur by overcoming our desire to indulge in momentary pleasures, then channeling those energies toward more lofty goals. If we had no inner desire to do the wrong things every day, our natures are such that we would not do nearly as much to perfect our character flaws and develop our eternity. For example, when given a choice between partying versus spending three hours developing patience and greater self-control, how many college students would choose the latter? How many people choose to work in a soup kitchen or visit residents of a nursing home instead of spending that time watching television, having a drink (or more), overeating, or gossiping? The harder we work to be less hedonistic, egocentric, and focused on short-term gratification, the more we strengthen the spiritual muscles that help us keep an eye on what is really important.

From Feeling a Lack to Spiritual Destruction

The serpent in the Garden of Eden was a model for how our negative inclination works. It makes us feel pained that something is missing, and then we want to fix that. Our good inclination will motivate us to fix the problem in the way that God wants it to be fixed, but our negative inclination will try its utmost to convince us to do otherwise. For example, a woman may be single and feel lonely. She really wants to get married and have children. She can dress very immodestly to attract men's attention, then have intimate relations with her dates because she hopes that this will get them to marry her. She doesn't realize how degrading, demoralizing, and counterproductive this is. If, instead, she dressed attractively but not in overly revealing clothes, and only dated men who respected her enough to develop a relationship leading to marriage, the outcome would be very different. The negative inclination convinces her to go a route that takes a terrible emotional, physical, and spiritual toll.

Criticizing Instead of Acting

Besides engaging in spiritually destructive behavior that we think will make us whole, we sometimes try to fix an imperfect world by criticizing others without doing anything to address the real problems. For example, an unhappy wife blames her husband for her lack of fulfillment; a worker blames his boss for his job dissatisfaction; newspaper reporters decry social ills without doing anything to make things better; and politicians enact laws that promote rights without responsibilities.

A better approach is to ask what God wants us to do. How would He want us to solve these problems?

The serpent's challenge to Eve reminds us that the quick fix might feel very right in the moment, but that the reward for listening to God is truly eternal.

Notes

1. Genesis 3:1.
2. Freud likely constructed some of his "innovative" psychological concepts, such as the id, the superego, and their constant conflict with one another from Judaism's ideas about the good and evil inclinations.
3. The Talmud (*Sanhedrin* 97a) teaches that the world will reach spiritual perfection by the Jewish year 6000. Whenever that perfection occurs, the Messianic age will begin. The Messiah will be a human being, born to human parents, who will be a descendant of King David. Such a person must be a righteous Jew who helps people realize that there is only one God who wants us to follow His will, as is stated in the Torah. He will be a Jewish leader whom all Jews accept, and he will lead the entire world to recognize the Almighty. A man in every generation is capable of being the Messiah. We will all know when the true Messiah arrives because after his arrival, everyone will be aware of, and be dedicated to, God. This means that all Gentiles will follow the Noahide laws, and all Jews will follow the Torah. Then, there will be no more wars, suffering, or immorality. Jews from around the world will return to Israel, Jerusalem will be their capital, and the third Temple will be built on the Temple Mount where the prior two Temples stood.

   There have been many failed potential messiahs throughout history, including Jewish kings, military leaders, and rabbis. When the Messiah finally arrives, everyone will know that he is the "real thing." By definition, someone cannot be the Messiah if the world is not ready for him.

   Early Christians took the Jewish concept of Messiah that predated Christianity by 1,300 years and created a novel idea. Since their leader didn't fulfill any of the age-old requirements of a Messiah, such as being a descendant of the Davidic dynasty, being a Jewish leader who was accepted by all Jews, bringing universal awareness of God and world peace, they originated the idea that he was a Messiah who would come a second time when the world would be ready for him. There is no basis in Jewish Scriptures or tradition for such a concept, so Christians mistranslated and took out of context many Biblical verses to bolster their new philosophy. They also reordered the Jewish Holy Books, added a few new books, and renamed the Jewish Holy Scriptures the "Old Testament" to fit with their new theology. For example, the Book of Malachi instead of Chronicles was put at the end of the Jewish Scriptures to make it seem that its last verse, which predicts the advent of Elijah the Prophet and the Messianic era, was predicting the birth of Jesus, whose story begins the New Testament.
4. Luzzatto, Moshe Chaim. *The Way of God*, I:3:1,2.
5. In ancient times, the people of the world were very drawn to idol worship. People should have used this drive to forge closeness with God. Instead of using their free will to direct their drives as our Creator intended, they misinterpreted and misdirected them. Idolatry was so alluring to the ancient Jews that most of them succumbed to its temptation. The Men of the Great Assembly (the Jewish legislative body) decided to fast and pray that the

Almighty abolish the temptation for idol worship, and He did. However, it came with a price tag. We no longer have the burning desire to sacrifice for and connect spiritually with our Creator as humanity once did. When the rabbis saw that their efforts to kill the drive for idolatry had succeeded, they prayed that God would likewise abolish the drive for immorality. When the rabbis saw that neither animals nor people had any desire to procreate, they asked that God only remove people's desire for incest, but that the rest of the sex drive's power stay intact (*Sanhedrin* 64a).

Temptation Beckons

Recognizing that Eve is a prototype for humanity in general, we can see ourselves and our responses to temptation in her story. Eve responded to the serpent's challenge:

> *"We may eat from the fruits of the tree of the Garden. And from the fruit of the tree that is in the middle of the Garden, God told us not to eat from it and not to touch it lest we die."*
>
> *And the serpent said to the woman, "You won't surely die. But God knows that in the day you eat of it, your eyes will be opened and you will be like God knowing good and evil."*
>
> *And the woman took from its fruit and she ate, and she gave it also to her husband with her and he ate.[1]*

The serpent began by asking the woman if God hadn't forbidden eating every fruit in the Garden of Eden (see previous section), knowing full well that only one fruit was off-limits. The serpent used this provocative remark to get Eve to talk to him.

Eve gave two noteworthy responses to the serpent: First, she identified the Tree of Knowledge as being the centerpiece of the Garden. The Torah had previously said that God put every good tree in the Garden, "and the Tree of Life in the midst of the Garden, and the Tree of Knowledge of Good and Evil."[2]

Even though both trees were in the center, the verse stresses that the Tree of *Life* was in the center of the Garden. The Tree of *Knowledge* was secondary.[3] Eve expressed a psychological shift by focusing on the centrality of the Tree of Knowledge, rather than on the Tree of Life, in the Garden. What was peripheral in her mind before was now the total focus of her attention.

Second, she told the serpent that she could neither eat from nor touch the Tree of Knowledge, lest she die. Yet God had never prohibited touching the tree. The Midrash says that Adam had not properly communicated to her God's command not to ingest the fruit. Instead, Adam had told her that she should not touch the tree nor eat from it. Touching something is a way to connect to it; Adam said not to touch the tree because he didn't want his wife connecting to it in any way, but he should have made it clear that it was his idea, not God's.

Error 1: Dignifying with a Response

Eve made several errors in responding to the serpent. First, she gave him credibility by dignifying him with a response. Once she started conversing with her negative inclination (represented by the serpent), Eve was trapped. She should have refused to talk to it because the only good way to respond to those who try to take us away from God is to move away from them. Giving real consideration to the serpent's words only magnified the allure of what was forbidden.

Error 2: Exaggerating Restrictions

Next, she made God's command sound worse than it was. This teaches that once we start questioning the divine will, we start to exaggerate how bad His restrictions are for us. This begins a slippery slope where, instead of getting objective answers from a trustworthy source about why the Almighty restricts us and why a particular behavior is spiritually destructive, we start to buy into the negative inclination's insistence that postponing or denying what we want must be bad.

Error 3: Doubting God's Word

The Midrash says that the serpent's next tactic was to push Eve into the tree, after which she saw that nothing happened upon contact.[4] She then began to doubt God's word and convinced herself that nothing bad would happen if she did what He forbade.

This scene graphically shows us how temptation works: We convince ourselves that we will never be punished for doing what's wrong. Our id tells us, "Do what makes you feel good. Do what you want, now. You deserve it. Nothing bad will happen. In fact, it will be good for you." We look at the short-term consequences of our behavior to reinforce what we want to believe. Of course, that can be very misleading because disobeying God always damages our soul and our connection to Him, but in ways that are usually not immediately apparent.

Bolt of Lightning

Many people have the childish notion that if eating forbidden food or gossiping or having non-marital sex were really wrong, God would strike us with a bolt of lightning when we did them. We can't judge whether something is right or wrong based only on tangible consequences. We have to trust that the One Above tells us how to live based on His knowledge of what is truly good or bad.

Error 4: Pursuing the Illusion

The serpent's next ploy was to tell Eve that God didn't want her to eat the forbidden fruit because doing so would make her as powerful as He. A Midrash says the serpent told Eve that eating the forbidden fruit had enabled God to create the world.[5] If she would eat the fruit, she could be equally powerful and creative.

The serpent's argument appealed to Eve's desire to be wise, powerful, creative, and independent of the Almighty.[6] She convinced herself that she could accomplish great things if she disobeyed Him, and that dependency on her Creator would impede her self-realization. As Eve convinced herself of the truth of the serpent's rhetoric, she exaggerated the benefits of eating the fruit. Suddenly, a mere tree was not only "good for eating, . . . desirable to the eyes, and . . . pleasant for discerning,"[7] it could even make her as wise, powerful, and creative as God, despite the fact that no fruit could possibly have been as wonderful as she imagined it would be. She then exercised her free will so she could be independent and avail herself of all of the goodies she believed the forbidden fruit could provide.

Unfortunately, it was only after disaster befell her that she realized that what seemed like such a good idea moments earlier was just an illusion.

Implications for Us

God gave us the desire to achieve, accomplish, and create, but this only has value if we express it in a way that also expresses our divinity. Freedom, power, artistic expression, money, intelligence, and careers are not intrinsically valuable. Their worth depends on how we use them. If we use freedom to make moral rather than immoral choices, it is good. If we use power to improve people's lives rather than exploit them, it is good. If we use careers and professions to make the world a better place, they are good. If any of these things cause us to become self-centered and lose sight of God's plans for how we should live, they are bad.

We may fool ourselves into believing we need things that aren't good for us, or that we do self-centered or immoral things for all of the right reasons. The workaholic insists that he is working so hard to give his family everything good, yet the spouse and children would rather have less money and more time with that person. We get physically involved with people with whom we shouldn't because we convince ourselves that we need or deserve such pleasure. We take things that don't belong to us because we convince ourselves that the big company or employer doesn't really care or won't really miss what we are taking.

We often do things that are immoral by exaggerating how great the money, love, appreciation, power, pleasure, or independence will make us feel. All too often, we find out the hard way that we only deceived ourselves when we see that the benefits of our misdeeds existed mostly in our imaginations.

Notes

1. Genesis 3:2-6. Since the Torah does not identify what the forbidden fruit was, the Talmud tried to do so. One opinion identified the forbidden "fruit" as wheat, since wheat is made into flour, and flour is made into bread. At one time, bread was the "staff of life." As such, it symbolizes knowledge. Since the first couple wanted to be as knowledgeable as God, the Sages suggested that wheat could have been the fateful "fruit" (*Genesis Rabbah* 15:7).

    The Sages also suggested figs, since Adam and Eve sought physical pleasure and figs are eaten only for their sweet taste, while wheat is usually eaten for nourishment. Grapes, whose wine is often used for sacrificial purposes, and the citron, which Jews take on the holiday of Tabernacles, might also have been the forbidden fruit.
2. Genesis 2:9.
3. There is a Kabbalistic idea that the Tree of Life was inside the trunk of the Tree of Knowledge, making the Tree of Life in the center as well.
4. *Genesis Rabbah* 19.
5. *Ibid.*
6. Samson Raphael Hirsch on Genesis 3:4.
7. Genesis 3:6.

Misery Loves Company

Once the first couple ate the forbidden fruit, they and their descendants were changed forever. Eating the forbidden fruit internalized in people a desire to flout God's will, along with feelings of jealousy, lust, and a desire for honor.[1] Before the sin, people didn't have these feelings. The first woman knew that she should stay away from the forbidden fruit and did not yet have an internalized desire to do what was wrong. Once the negative inclination was no longer an abstract idea, but part of her very self, jealousy, lust, and a desire for honor would infect humanity and bring many people to their downfall.

Once Eve sinned, her negative inclination overpowered her, and she no longer saw her husband as part of herself. Once we stop identifying people as part of "us," we often feel threatened by them. In Eve's case, she realized that she would die and Adam would survive. She couldn't bear the idea that he would remarry and love a second wife. Thus, she offered Adam the fruit, thinking, "If we die, we will both die. If we live, we will both live."[2] The serpent had made his overture to Eve because he believed that if she were corrupted, she would also corrupt her husband. Were that to happen, the serpent's mission would be an unqualified success.

Eve understood that Adam's Achilles' heel was his desire for closeness with her. After all, his initial loneliness prompted him to want a wife. Rather than admit her wrongdoing and do what she could to fix it, her jealousy prompted her to get her husband to share her fate. How true it is that misery loves company!

We can understand why Eve tried to bring Adam down, but why did the uncorrupted Adam give in to her?

One explanation is that Adam had been so lonely before he received a soul mate, and he could not imagine getting another wife since there were no other women in the world.[3] While Eve apparently thought that the Almighty might give him a second wife, she convinced Adam that God would not create another woman for him.[4] Adam was so afraid of being alone, he didn't trust God to give him what he needed. This means his fear of loneliness was more real to him than his belief that the One who gave him a wife in the first place would surely take care of him.

Implications for Us

Adam could not imagine living alone forever, so he agreed to stay with Eve and share her destiny. How often do we do the same by acting in ways that degrade us or by getting into destructive relationships rather than face being alone?

Rationalizing Our Failings

We sometimes think that, had we been in the Garden of Eden, we wouldn't have disobeyed God. Yet we rationalize our failing the spiritual tests that are tailor-made for us. Doing what our Creator wants is sometimes emotionally painful. It can feel more comfortable and less threatening to accept our shortcomings and stop trying to improve than it does to strive to be better and sometimes fail. Some people even try to legitimize their moral failures by joining social or political movements that support their behavior and discredit anyone who disagrees with them.

Belittling Strivers

Instead of admitting our mistakes and resolving to improve, we may speak cynically or derogatorily about those who strive for moral excellence. We regard such people as fanatics or as being rigid or old-fashioned instead of admiring their moral rectitude. We may focus only on their shortcomings (real or imagined), stereotype them, or even try to make them fail so that the gap between them and us is less glaring.

When we aren't living up to God's will for us, we may need to set realistic small goals, change slowly, and give ourselves credit for moving in the right direction. Sabotaging others or ourselves when we fail is the worst thing we can do.

Notes

1. *Genesis Rabbah* 14:4.
2. *Genesis Rabbah* 20:8.
3. Rabbi Dessler on Genesis 3 advanced a different interpretation. He suggested that Adam ate the fruit because Adam believed that he would be spiritually greater if he internalized a negative inclination and then overcame it. He didn't feel that spiritually developing himself was much of an accomplishment without an internal negative inclination to challenge him.
4. *Genesis Rabbah* 19:5.

Truth and Consequences

Tragically, the first couple disobeyed God shortly after He created them. They thought that using their judgment about how to live would lead to wonderful rewards. Instead, they then had to confront the enormity of the ruin they had caused. Genesis describes how they, as prototypical people, responded when they were confronted with their misbehavior, and how the Almighty reacted in turn. After Adam and Eve sinned, God asked Adam,

> *"Have you eaten from the tree that I commanded you not to eat from?"*
> *And the man said, "The woman whom You gave to be with me, she gave me from the tree and I ate."*
> *And the Lord God said to the woman, "What is this that you have done?"*
> *And the woman said, "The serpent beguiled me and I ate."[1]*

Rather than accept responsibility for their wrongdoing, the first man and woman blamed someone else for their misdeeds. When they refused to repent and ask for God's forgiveness, He responded as follows:

> *To the woman He said, "I will make your birth pain very severe. You will have sorrow when you give birth to children. Your desire will be to your husband and he will rule over you."*
> *To the man He said, "Because you listened to your wife's voice and ate from the tree which I commanded you not to eat from it, the earth will be cursed for you. In sorrow you will eat from it all the days of your life. It will grow you thorns and thistles and you will eat the grass of the field. By the sweat of your nose you will eat bread*

until you return to the earth because you were taken from
there because you are dust and you shall return to dust."[2]

How could God mete out such terrible punishments for simply eating a fruit? To understand how the punishment fit the crime, let's learn more about the original divine plan for humanity.

Disconnecting Mortal from Immortal

When God warned that eating the forbidden fruit would be deadly, it was not because He would kill Adam and Eve, but because wrongdoing automatically disconnects the body from its life-giving soul. The Almighty created human beings with an immortal soul so that people could live forever. However, they would only live forever if their bodies did God's will. This is because everything physical, even the smallest elementary particles, are limited and destined to decay. Once we disconnect our physical self from our immortal soul, the soul can't infuse the body with the eternity that our Creator wants us to have. That makes it inevitable that someone who sins will die.

Adam and Eve caused their own demise by eating the forbidden fruit. By severing the perfect link between body and soul, their personal desires overrode their spiritual, immortal side. Death is inevitable when we betray our soul by indulging our body and its wishes as an end in itself.

Custom Punishment

The Torah defines sin as any action, word, or thought that distances us from the Almighty. Therefore, an element of punishment is inherent in any sin because having a less-intimate relationship with our Creator pains our souls. In addition, the Almighty metes out punishments that help us rectify what we did wrong. These punishments are custom-designed to spiritually fix each failing.

Our greatest reward for doing God's will is the pleasure that our souls experience from their intimacy with our Creator here and in the next world.

When the soul leaves this world, it gets punished for all of the bad things that the person did; then it gets rewarded for all of the good things that the person did. The Talmud describes this process:

> *When a person departs for his eternal home, all of his deeds are enumerated before him. He is told, "You did such-and-such in this place on that day."*
>
> *He replies, "Yes."*
>
> *They say to him, "Sign."*
>
> *And he signs. . . . He even admits the justice of the verdict and says, "You have judged me well."*[3]

"Hell" is our realization in the afterlife of how we squandered opportunities for spiritual growth, hurt people, and betrayed our Creator during our time on earth. The "flames of hell" are our burning with shame over our failure to be what we could have been and the pain of realizing how we misused opportunities to create true goodness.

Rabbi Aryeh Kaplan described this as follows:

> *Imagine standing naked before God, with your memory wide open, completely transparent without any*[thing] *. . . to diminish its force. You will remember everything you ever did. . . . The memory of every good deed would be the sublimest of pleasures. . . . But your memory will also be open to all the things of which you are ashamed. They cannot be rationalized away or dismissed. You will be facing yourself, fully aware of the consequences of all your deeds. We all know the terrible shame and humiliation when one is caught in the act of doing something wrong. Imagine being caught . . . with no place to escape. . . .*[4]

"Heaven" is the eternal pleasure we enjoy from having used our time on earth meaningfully and in ways that brought us close to our Creator. Our Sages expressed this by saying, "Better one moment of pleasure in the afterlife than all of the pleasures of this world."[5]

We often think that "Heaven" is what our senses or ego tell us feel best now, and "Hell" is foregoing those gratifications. Just like the person who goes to a weekend party and drinks only "a little bit" to feel better, we often don't know where pursuing what we want will take us. What is certain is that, if pursuing our desires conflicts with God's plan, His ideas are always right and our contradictory ones will bring us to ruin. The morning after, we will always have a "hangover"!

Implications for Us

The stories of Adam and Eve teach us that everything God tells us to do, or to refrain from doing, is only for our benefit. Like a loving parent, He has no desire to impose authority on us or punish us. He would like us to live in the way that ultimately benefits us most. All of His commandments are designed to benefit our souls and to help us feel His love. When we go off track, though, He must respond in ways that may feel painful so that the world's purpose can be fulfilled.

Every moral challenge is an opportunity for us to grow closer to our Creator. Overcoming those challenges often requires us to say "no" to things that would make us feel good for a moment, yet which wouldn't bring us true dignity and purpose. We need to train ourselves to look past the disappointment or struggle of the moment to the ultimate good that we build by obeying our Creator. When we slip and make mistakes, the best thing we can do is to honestly admit what we did wrong, ask for God's forgiveness, redress the wrong if possible, and then try to get ourselves back on track as quickly as possible.

Notes
1. Genesis 3:11-13.
2. Genesis 3:16-19.
3. *Taanit* 11a.
4. In *If You Were God: Three Works by Aryeh Kaplan*, Mesorah, Brooklyn, 1983, pp. 23-37.
5. *Ethics of the Fathers* 4:29.

The Power of Words

Before the first woman sinned, she was called "*ishah*" ("the woman of spiritual excellence"). After the woman failed in her primary role as a helper to her husband, she had to have a new role, so her husband renamed her:

> *And he* [Adam] *called the name of his wife Chavah, because she was the mother of all living.*[1]

Her new name, *Chavah*, retains the Hebrew letter *heh*, which represents half of God's Name. Had Adam lived up to his spiritual calling he could have become a man of spiritual excellence (*ish*). That name contains the Hebrew letter *yud,* which, together with the *heh* from *Chavah*, would have completed God's Name. It is now poignantly missing because the Almighty's Name was no longer complete. It was broken, so to speak, by Adam and Eve's unfaithfulness to their Creator. *Chavah*, or Eve, will now pass on her divine mission to her descendants, but will no longer be able to fulfill it herself.

When God initially made the woman, He intended her to be Adam's partner in perfecting the world. After she sinned, being a mother became her primary role. Prior to the sin, being Adam's partner in perfecting the world was her primary role, and being a mother was a secondary one.[2] The antidote for bringing death into the world was to physically and spiritually nurture future generations who would now need to morally perfect the world.[3]

In Aramaic, the word *Chavah* also means "conversation."[4] Chavah used her power of speech to entice her husband to sin. The Talmud says that God gave women greater linguistic abilities than men so that women would use these qualities to nurture people and perfect the world.[5] It made sense that after her sin, woman was renamed to reflect the power that she wielded in potentially doing good with her words.

Implications for Us

One of the most important gifts we have is the power of speech. We should never trivialize it by gossiping, prattling for no real purpose, cursing, or using coarse language. Because the power of speech has such tremendous potential for doing good, it has an equal and opposite potential for causing destruction. That is why some people abuse this amazing gift by using words to manipulate people, lie, slander, or hurt people's feelings. The ultimate purpose of speech is to bring us and others closer to God through prayer and learning the Torah, bringing peace between people, offering kindness and comfort, and the like.

Unfortunately, there is a misguided notion that we should indiscriminately share our feelings with others, regardless of their impact. We need to refrain from communicating feelings that can only destroy our relationships or have a devastating impact on others. If we can't speak constructively, silence is best.

Some ground rules for constructive criticism: We should never criticize others when we are very angry, lest we convey the wrong message. We should preface and follow any criticism with a compliment. The criticism itself should be given when the other person is listening and is receptive. (If the other person is not receptive, then criticism is pointless, or even harmful.) Criticism should be brief and address a behavior, not globally attack a person. It should also be followed by a recommendation for what a preferred behavior would be.

Adam's renaming the first woman *Chavah* reminds us that one of the most important abilities we can develop is communicating constructively so that we bring out the best in others and in ourselves.

Notes

1. Genesis 3:20.
2. The fact that her initial primary role was as Adam's partner doesn't mean that she didn't have her own intrinsic worth. It meant that both she and Adam needed to work in concert to use their individual identities to bring the world to spiritual perfection.
3. Malbim on Genesis 3:20.
4. *Genesis Rabbah* on 3:20.
5. The Talmud (*Kiddushin* 49b) expresses this idea as, "God put ten measures of speech into the world. Women were given nine of them."

Sin and Punishment

Every sin causes some spiritual damage that needs to be fixed, and the Almighty always designs a punishment that fits the crime. After Adam and Eve ate the forbidden fruit, each had to fix the damage caused by their disobedience in different ways. We will soon identify the real nature of each crime and punishment.

After Adam and Eve ate the forbidden fruit, they tried to hide from their Creator. God asked Adam why he was hiding, and Adam gave a ridiculous excuse. When the Lord gave him a second chance to admit his wrongdoing, Adam still didn't accept responsibility for his misdeed, and he blamed Eve and the Almighty, "The woman whom You gave to be with me, she gave me from the tree and I ate."[1]

When God asked Eve what she had done, hoping that she would own up to her misdeed, she blamed her failing on the serpent: "[He] seduced me, and I ate."[2]

After Adam and Eve refused to admit their wrongdoing and repent, their Creator changed them. For example, prior to sinning, pregnancy and birth were easy and quick, and the man did not have to work hard to procure food.[3] Now matters were different.

> To the woman He said, "I will make great your pain and your pregnancy. You will have sorrow when you give birth to children. Your desire will be to your husband and he will rule over you."[4]
>
> To the man He said, "Because you listened to your wife's voice and ate from the tree which I commanded you not to eat from it, the earth will be cursed for you. In sorrow you will eat from it all the days of your life. It will grow you thorns and thistles and you will eat the grass of the field. By the sweat of your nose you will eat bread until you return to the earth because you were taken from there because you are dust and you shall return to dust."[5]

The above passage calls into question what God's "anger" is all about. When the Torah says that God became "angry," it means that man's behavior did not allow Him to give of His blessing. Our Creator never has human emotions such as anger, and Divine punishment is never an act of revenge. The Almighty punishes us to educate us and/or give us a chance to rectify our shortcomings.

Thus, after Eve sinned, He changed her in ways that would allow her to rectify (1) her attempt to stay independent of God and (2) the spiritual damage she had caused.

Control vs. Calling to God

The essence of Eve's sin was that she tried to control Adam and be independent of her Maker. Eve was now going to enter into relationships that she could not fully control: her relationship with her husband, becoming and being pregnant, giving birth, and raising children. A primary reason that women feel that they do not have control over their lives is their inability to control so much of what happens to them in relation to people in their lives. Eve's difficulties with pregnancy, childbirth, and raising children[6] were designed to motivate her to call out to her Creator and ask Him for help. Seeing that she was not in control would make her realize how dependent she really was on her Maker and have a close relationship with Him. It also motivated her (and her female descendants, since she had all of their souls within her) to make the One Above central to their lives and pray for His help, direction, and support.

"Great pain" occurs when parents raise their offspring. This especially occurs when children mimic their parents' shortcomings and character flaws. Parents are terribly pained when they see their children doing what the parents do, rather than doing what the parents say to do. This phenomenon is supposed to get parents to improve themselves in order to set a good example for their children.

Marital Motivation

That a woman's passion will be toward her husband, yet he will dominate her, means that a woman will long to be with her husband during times of separation, yet she can only have relations when he wants intimacy. Women are supposed to encourage their husbands to be close to them using positive means, rather than using destructive manipulation as Eve did to convince Adam that if he wanted intimacy with her, he would have to share her fate.

The Talmud says that after her sin, God made Eve and her female descendants want to stay home.[7] This means that women would be torn between their multiple roles. In today's world, women have to choose between having careers, getting more education, making the community a better place, developing and nurturing themselves outside of their homes, and/or staying home with their families. Women want to create worlds as God did, yet they will feel conflicted about how best to use their intellects, emotions, time, and talents.

While the women's movement stressed education and career over all other potential choices, many observant Jewish women spend the majority of their time and energy raising families. That is not to say that they don't get an education or work outside the home, but their lives often revolve for many years around raising children. While being a mother has been devalued in the Western world, one of the greatest forms of creativity is giving birth to a human being and helping him or her develop. While this is enormously gratifying, it is also incredibly demanding and difficult. Other projects have a discrete beginning and end, which sometimes feels more gratifying than the unending task of making a home and raising children. There is almost never a time when a woman can say that she has successfully completed childrearing. Yet if she sees that she raised children who try to fulfill their spiritual potential and make the world a better place, she feels a sense of achievement that is unparalleled. In this way, many women can take Eve's changes and use the ideas underlying them to realize their potentials in our time.

Implications for Us

The Almighty views women and men as being equally important in morally perfecting the world. While God has neither a body nor a gender, He has both masculine and feminine attributes that we are supposed to emulate.

Some people have used the story of Eve's sin and punishment as a pretext for devaluing and oppressing females. Genesis tells us that both men and women have potential greatness as well as potential shortcomings. Our Creator gave each sex different ways to realize those potentials, including commandments that protect us from falling into moral traps.

Judaism values the importance of having two-parent families and raising well-adjusted, moral children. Parents who take their role seriously are nothing less than God's partners in creating worlds. When they do this, they help fix the sin in the Garden of Eden and bring the world back to Paradise.

Notes
1. Genesis 3:11.
2. Genesis 3:13.
3. *Eruvin* 100b details the ten ways by which the man, the woman, and the serpent were each affected.
4. Genesis 3:16.
5. Rashi interprets "increase your pain" to refer to the difficulties a woman undergoes when she raises children.
6. Genesis 3:18-19. If women wish to avail themselves of anesthesia and modern medical techniques to make childbirth easier, they are welcome to do so.
7. *Eruvin* 100b.

Adam's Changes

Eve sinned first, and Genesis delineates her punishment before that of her husband. Now that we have explored her sin and God's response, we can examine why Adam was punished by having to work hard for a living and by becoming mortal. His sin had at least three aspects:

1. **Not trusting God.** Adam didn't trust that God had provided him with everything he needed. He didn't believe that, if his Creator had forbidden him a single fruit, that fruit must not have been good for him.

   Since the true Judge punishes us "measure for measure," the corrective for Adam's lack of trust began by making man's life materially uncertain. Adam could no longer rely on the Almighty's agents—nature, the ground, and the trees—to provide him with food. The first man would now have to till the soil, plant crops, weed, prune, and hope that there would be favorable weather and rain to nurture what he had planted. After all his backbreaking work, plant diseases, floods, drought, strong winds, unusual temperatures, or pests could ruin the fruits of his labor. His new circumstances would, hopefully, continually remind him that material prosperity comes from the Director of Nature.[1] God wanted man to realize that he can't rely on his own efforts alone to get what he needs. Realizing our limitations should motivate us to ask our Creator to provide, thereby cementing an ongoing closeness between us.

   Just as Eve's female descendants have to rectify Eve's failures, Adam's male descendants have to fix his. This is because he had within him all of the male souls that will ever exist, and his failures metaphysically affected all of them. Today, work is still supposed to motivate men to feel dependent on God for their success and encourage them to realize that everything they do is in partnership with the One Above. The vagaries of nature (or the job market) encourage men to realize that the Almighty is the ultimate Provider and Comptroller. By praying to God for material success and acknowledging that one is never "self-made," men can develop the humility that will allow them to trust and depend on their Creator in ways that Adam did not. Having a close relationship with God as a result of working hard rectifies Adam's sin and furthers the Almighty's purposes for the world.

We have to work hard to earn a living yet always know that our success depends upon God. A surgeon, for example, can't sit back and expect the Almighty to pick up a scalpel and do surgery on his patients. He must make every effort to keep abreast of the latest techniques and knowledge and do the best he can to make the operation a success. Yet, having done that, he must know that the outcome is not up to him. While many people want to become self-made men and women and take all of the credit for their achievements, we need to remember that we can only make the effort; God determines the results.

2. **Not being grateful.** Adam wasn't grateful for all of the fruits of Paradise he had received without any effort. God put the entire world at his disposal and gave him a soul mate, yet Adam blamed God for giving him a wife! The remedy for Adam's lack of appreciation was the need to work very hard for what he previously got with no effort. Only then would he truly appreciate what he received.

3. **Preferring to be with his wife rather than obey God.** Work would take him away from his wife, making it impossible for him to be with her as often as he otherwise would have.[2]

Implications for Us

We can learn from Adam the importance of appreciating and acknowledging what we receive and to fight our tendency to take things for granted. God gives us a variety of tasty, nutritious, beautiful, and aromatic foods to eat. We don't even have to personally toil to grow them. He gives us varied clothes that we don't personally weave or sew from raw materials. He gives us healthy bodies that function and allow us to see, hear, taste, touch, smell, and move. He gives us homes with heat, clean water, indoor plumbing, and modern conveniences. We take all of these for granted, yet they are truly privileges that the majority of the world's people do not yet enjoy.

We should not only appreciate our blessings every day, we should thank the One who gave them. Focusing on what we have instead of on what we lack helps us enjoy life and not feel overwhelmed by difficulties.

Adam's story also reminds us that even unpleasant situations can bring us closer to the Almighty. When we act improperly, we should take responsibility for our misdeeds and not repeat them. Blaming others or attributing such problems to bad luck will only cause us to suffer more as we resent the consequences of our actions instead of growing from them.

Notes

1. Ancient societies understood very well the uncertainty of agricultural success. They worshipped a panoply of idols to try to guarantee what their efforts alone could not. Many farmers today and people who live in third-world countries still appreciate God's central role in providing whatever is necessary to insure the success of their crops.

2. This was also a punishment for Eve and for her descendants. Women complain that Adam's descendants spend too much time absorbed with work instead of spending time with their wives and children!

Clothing

Juxtaposed between the stories about the first couple's creation and sin are descriptions of their state of dress. Since the Torah is not a fashion handbook, what are we supposed to learn from these seemingly superfluous verses?

First, Genesis informs us that when Adam and Eve were created,

> *the two of them were naked, the man and his wife, and they were not ashamed.*[1]

After they sinned and were punished,

> *the Lord God made the man and his wife tunics of animal skin* [or] *and He dressed them.*[2]

The Hebrew words for "skin" and "light" are very similar. The Sages say that Adam and Eve wore "garments of light" (*or*) prior to sinning.[3] Rather than having normal physical bodies, they radiated the spiritual light of the divine Presence within them. When they looked at each other, they saw only this light rather than flesh.[4]

Being naked is not embarrassing as long as we use our bodies only to elevate the soul. Once Adam and Eve sinned by using their bodies in self-centered ways instead of using them to fulfill their divine missions, the Almighty clothed them with animal skins, also called *or* in Hebrew (but spelled differently from the word for "light"). The play on the word *or* expressed the idea that sin blocked Adam and Eve from seeing inner divinity radiating through their skin. Although bodies are supposed to be garments for the soul, the skin garments were reminders that Adam and Eve now saw their animal selves in their flesh.

Now that we understand why the Almighty made garments of skin for people, we can explore the symbolism in the type of animal whose skin was used. One idea is that it was a *tachash*. When God told the Israelites to build the Tabernacle in the wilderness, he directed them to cover it with *tachash* skin. We don't know what a *tachash* is because it is extinct now. We only know that it was an animal of "many colors."

The Tabernacle that the Israelites built after they left Egypt, and which they used until King Solomon built the First Temple, symbolized the human being. Its vessels paralleled human limbs and organs, while its covering of *tachash* fur symbolized skin. The *tachash* skin's many colors made it impossible to see what color it really was. This reminded people of our difficulty in seeing reality clearly and of how we can confuse what seems appealing with what is truly good. Clothing Adam and Eve with *tachash* skin symbolized their disobedience-caused confusion about what was right and wrong.

Another opinion was that Adam's and Eve's clothing was made from a leviathan, an enormous whale-like creature.[5] When these enormous sea creatures were created, God killed the female leviathan and salted it to preserve it as a reward for the feast of the righteous in the World-to-Come. At this future feast, righteous people will also eat of this and sit in the shade of the leviathan's skin.[6]

This allegory can mean the following: We become righteous by discerning how God wants us to act, then doing only what He tells us is right. Fish symbolize physical desire, and fish skin symbolizes subduing physical desire.[7] Thus, the souls of righteous people will be rewarded by experiencing pleasure (allegorized as eating) when they see how subduing their desires (the shade of the skin) continually affirms the way God wants them to live. The *tachash* represents our confusion about how we should live; the reward of the leviathan represents our mastering that confusion.

Implications for Us

The fashion industry and media try to determine the images we project to others. What do these images say about us? Do they reflect who we truly are and who we should be?

Judaism says that we should project images of what's true, lasting, and real about ourselves to the outside world. Our true essence is our divine image within, not the contours of our flesh. While we should dress attractively, we should not trivialize ourselves by dressing in ways that mostly try to get attention.

Jewish law requires people to dress modestly to remind us that what is most essential about us (our souls) is covered (by the body). The body, which is supposed to be a vehicle of the soul, is dressed to remind us that the body is a means to a spiritual end—and should not be seen or used as an end in itself.

The dress code for Jews is more stringent for women than for men. It is geared toward helping women appear attractive, but not attracting. This is because men are more likely to relate superficially to women than vice versa. When a woman dresses modestly, it is easier for others to focus on her spiritual/moral/inner transcendent self.

Women might balk at the idea of covering body parts that are beautiful and have sensual allure. However, while modest attire may get less sensually oriented attention, it allows women to retain their dignity and to help outsiders focus on what's real and worthwhile instead of flaunting what's skin-deep and shallow. When modestly dressed women do get noticed, they are more likely to be taken seriously than if they were exposing themselves.

The clothes we wear reflect what we consider important about ourselves. Do we value our moral character more than our wealth and our sex appeal? Do we try to hide our ages because our life experiences and knowledge are not as valued as smooth skin? Do we believe that people won't find us worthwhile if we don't loudly advertise our presence? The more we develop our Godly essence and feel good about who we truly are inside, the less we need to impress the world by our physical features.

Notes

1. Genesis 1:25.
2. Genesis 3:21.
3. Munk, Eliyahu (ed.). *Shney Luchot Habrit.* Jerusalem, 1992, p. 37. See also Elie Munk, *Call of the Torah,* (Vol. 1), New York, Feldheim, 1980, p. 98-99, for a description of the original nature of people.
4. The Sfat Emmet on Genesis 3:21.
5. The Talmud (*Bava Batra* 74b) says that God made the great sea creatures—the leviathan and its mate—on the fifth day of creation. God neutered the male and killed the female and salted it for the righteous so that the leviathan pair would not procreate and destroy the world.
6. *Bava Batra* 75a.
7. This interpretation was expressed by Rabbi Uziel Milevsky, zt"l, in a taped lecture circa 1980s at Ohr Samayach Yeshiva in Jerusalem.

Bad is Very Good

Because Genesis describes how people corrupted the world that God made, we might wonder why the Almighty allowed this to happen. At the end of the sixth day of Creation, as God surveys His world, He comments, "And behold, it was very good."[1] This contrasts with the other days,[2] when God surveys His creations and says, "It was good." Various Midrashim[3] explain that "very good" refers to those things that were created at the end of the sixth day that we normally assume are bad, such as death, punishment, and suffering. These made God's world "*very* good." This seems perplexing.

The Talmud says Rabbi Levi explained that "and behold it was very good" means that God saw the totality of His creations (which people can't do) and was aware of how every detail could both conceal and reveal His Presence. Events that may lead us to believe that there is no purpose to life—or that can interfere with our relating to a loving, caring God—can also help us search for and find Him. Things that we perceive as being good, together with those that we think of as bad, are actually very good *in toto*. While tragedies such as death can lead some people to conclude that there is no purpose to life, it encourages others to seek deeper meaning. For example, the majority of parents whose children die become more religious as a result, while only a minority alienate themselves from God.[4]

As long as people are comfortable, they may think that the purpose of life is to achieve sensual or material pleasure and comfort. Tragedies can shake us up and make us wonder what life is really all about. They can remind us to be more serious about living for eternally meaningful goals. They can also encourage some people to look for a God who was not previously important to them.

A world without ultimate reward and punishment for the soul, without suffering, and without the possibility of evil, would not give us meaningful moral choices. We can only have free will if life is sometimes painful and seemingly unfair events sometimes happen. If it were obvious that a loving God runs the world, and our living by His rules brought only goodness and reward, we would do the right things for the wrong reasons. We would follow His rules only to avoid punishment or to be rewarded, not because we want a relationship with Him.

God's greatest goodness is to let us make truly meaningful choices, including making constructive responses to painful situations that conceal His Presence. These challenges are *very* good because they are the very tools that we use to make life purposeful.

Implications for Us

The Creation story teaches us that potential good is inherent in every seemingly bad event. A couple that suffers from infertility, or a woman who miscarries, might later appreciate the birth of a child as the miracle that it truly is. Someone who loses a job or undergoes financial hardship might realize that a loving family and good friends are more important than material possessions. Someone who has cancer might live life with an intensity that was formerly missing.[5]

We grow most through experiences of discomfort and challenge that we would never choose to undergo. The fact that we have these experiences tells us that the Almighty believes it necessary for us to weather these storms. Our best possible response is to turn to our Creator for support and guidance as we search for meaning, learn from these painful events, and change constructively through them.

Part II: The Garden of Eden - Bad is Very Good

Notes

1. Genesis 1:31.
2. Described in Genesis 1:4, 10, 11, 12, 18, 21, 25.
3. For example, *Genesis Rabbah* 9:5, 7 11.
4. Klass, Dennis. *Spiritual Lives of Bereaved Parents*. London, Brunner-Routledge, 1999.
5. There are many reasons why people suffer. For a fuller discussion of this topic, see Lisa Aiken, *Why Me, God? A Jewish Guide to Coping with Suffering*. Northvale, NJ, Jason Aronson, 1996.

The Sabbath

As the six days of Creation ended, the Master of the World invested the world with its soul, the Sabbath:

> *And the heavens and the earth and all of their hosts were finished* [vayechulu]. *And on the seventh day God finished all of the creative activity that He had made. And He let go on the seventh day of all the creativity that He had made. And God blessed the seventh day and sanctified it because He let go on* [that day] *from all the creativity that God created to be made.*[1]

Shabbat, Soul of the World

Just as a person needs a soul, so does the world. This is why God created the Sabbath as soon as He finished making the physical world. When we connect to God on this day of rest, we activate the world's soul and become His partners in creating and maintaining the universe.

Physical World's Stages of Creation

The first Sabbath occurred in two stages:

1. **God stopped creating the physical world.** If God hadn't stopped building the physical world after the first six days of Creation, nature and materialism would have loomed so large that they would have completely dissuaded people from looking for a spiritual Being behind the world.[2]

2. **God gave people a special opportunity and desire to find Him on the Sabbath.** *Vayechulu* is an unusual word to convey that God "completed the heavens and the earth and all of their hosts."[3] *Vayigmiru* would be used were the verse simply telling us that He finished creating the world. *Vayechal*, a word that comes from the same root as

vayechulu, is used by the Torah in describing another event: the completion of the Tabernacle built by the Israelites in the Sinai desert. The Tabernacle was a place where one most easily saw the Divine Presence. We can infer from this that the Sabbath likewise makes the world a place conducive to finding the Divine Presence.

After God made the Sabbath, it was as if the Creator had endowed people with a special ability to see that He made everything and that a divine plan underlay all of Creation.

A Physical World Worth Celebrating

Vayechulu is similar to the Hebrew word *kallah*, meaning "bride." A Midrash analogizes God's finishing His physical creation of the world to a king who erected a wedding canopy without a bride in sight. Just as wedding trappings without a bride are meaningless, so is a physical world without the Sabbath as its Godly emblem. This is why the Sabbath is considered a special sign of the bond between the Jews and the Almighty. When we observe the laws that honor and protect the sanctity of the Sabbath, we testify that the Creator made a purposeful world, and we show that we want to live up to its purpose.

Yearning

Rabbi Chaim ben Attar said that the word *vayechulu* comes from the same root as the Hebrew word for yearning.[4] "*Vayechulu* the heavens and earth" means that God gave each part of the universe a deep and constant yearning to connect to Him and receive His spiritual light. God reveals Himself and enables us to receive His light more on the Sabbath than on weekdays. Immersing ourselves in the Sabbath liberates our souls from their worldly confines and makes us yearn to come closer to Him. That, in turn, gives our lives meaning.

Empty vs. Full Vessels

Vayechulu is also related to the Hebrew world *keli*, which means "vessel." A Midrash explains that the heavens and earth were "vessels" that revealed God's Presence only after He made the Sabbath. Without a Sabbath that encouraged people to discern the world's ultimate meaning and purpose, the world was no better off with lots of creations than it was without them. The Sabbath gave the physical world purpose and meaning.

Hosts

That heaven and earth were created with all of their "hosts" means that every part of Creation is necessary for our searching for, finding, and serving God. Nothing that He created is superfluous or without potential spiritual value. We simply have to use it for these intended purposes.

"Hosts" also means "armies." Each person is an indispensable soldier in the Almighty's army. We each have a unique role to play in His cosmic plan, and no one else can make the spiritual contributions that each one of us was put here to make.

Menuchah vs. Materialism

The Torah says that God completed all of His creative activity on the seventh day, even though the material world was finished at the end of the sixth day. What did He add to the world on the seventh day? Inner peace—*menuchah*. There is an expression, "When the Sabbath comes, inner peace comes." The physical world cannot be complete without the spiritual peace that the Sabbath brings.

People who focus on material things can never truly feel at peace. They worry about keeping what they have, getting more, and having less than others. We can only have inner peace when we are satisfied with what we have and with who we are. That happens when we end our preoccupation with material desires and objects and instead connect to our souls. Everything physical is finite and temporary. We can only view our lives properly by focusing at least one day a week on what's real, lasting, and eternal—our relationship with God, His Torah, our appreciating and nurturing the divine image in others, and our spiritual development.

Our souls want us to let go of the world's trappings and find serenity with our Maker. We lose sight of the true purpose of life when we focus on, and invest ourselves in, the physical world as an end in itself. The physical world should be a means for rectifying and developing our souls and the world. We were not created to amass material things and invest ourselves in self-serving pleasures. As we shall soon see, pleasures and possessions are supposed to be means to spiritual ends.

We make the Sabbath holy by withdrawing somewhat from the physical world and refraining from many forms of creative activity. This mirrors how the Almighty stopped creating the physical world on the Sabbath.

Spiritualizing the Physical

Since the purpose of life is to spiritualize the physical, we use physical pleasures—eating, drinking, and even marital relations—to enhance our relationship with God on the Sabbath.

Every week, from sundown Friday until nightfall (about 45 minutes after sunset) Saturday, God infuses spiritual energy into the world that helps us clarify what is real and important. This helps us fulfill the true purpose of Creation—to find Him behind the masks of the material world.

On Shabbat, we reaffirm our soul's connection to our Creator by spiritualizing the physical world through prayer, Torah study, and Sabbath rituals. These rituals include –

Candles. We light candles at least 18 minutes before sunset Friday afternoon, bringing peace and serenity to the home on Friday night.

Special Meals. We enjoy three meals with special bread and especially delicious food that we don't normally eat the rest of the week.[5]

Quality Time. We spend quality time with our family and guests. Friday night is also a special time for a married couple to have physical relations.[6]

Prayers and Songs. We sanctify Friday dinner and Saturday lunch by first saying *Kiddush*, a prayer testifying to the day's holiness, over grape juice or wine.[7] At each of the three Sabbath meals, we sing songs that sanctify the day by recalling its purpose. We begin and end each meal by thanking our Host.

On Saturday, we spend a lot of time praying and studying Torah. When we pray, we talk to God. When we learn Torah, God speaks to us.

Implications for Us

The Sabbath reminds us that the physical world is only a means to a spiritual end. Many people mistakenly think that Saturday is supposed to be a day to have fun, go to the beach, movies, restaurants, or the mall, or do laundry and run errands. Others think that its true purpose is to replenish ourselves emotionally and physically so that we can work the rest of the week. Its real purpose is to reorient ourselves so that we will use the weekdays to continually search for the Divine Presence that we find most easily on the Sabbath.

God wants us to enjoy physical pleasures in His Presence. The Sabbath reminds us of what is really important. If we all spent one day a week reflecting upon our relationship to the world, to people, and to our Creator, and then spent the next six days living in ways that respect those relationships, what a wonderful world it would be.

Universal Studios

Universal Studios is a great way to learn that, although seeing is believing, our perceptions can be totally false. This wonderful tourist attraction shows visitors a Western town from the 1800s, a section of Wall Street, bridges that collapse, buildings that blow up, the parting of the Red Sea, and even an earthquake inside a San Francisco subway. It all seems totally real until we look behind the scenes and see that it's all an illusion! The buildings are facades, the rumblings and crashings are done with special effects, the fires are controlled explosions, and the parting of the Red Sea is merely a rising platform in a holding tank. Once you see how these places and events are constructed and engineered, it clarifies how illusory "reality" can be.

Universal Studios is a metaphor for our world. We are sure that ultimate reality is what we see, touch, smell, and hear. But these perceptions often mask the truest reality—the spiritual sparks that vivify us and the world and that connect us to our Creator. He gave us a weekly Sabbath to remind us that the physical world is simply a facade that masks the spiritual world.

The Sabbath Psalm

Tashuv/**Repentance.** As soon as Adam ate the forbidden fruit, he felt the horror of what he had done. When he experienced his first evening, he assumed that it was the final dark curtain coming down on the world, and he feared there would be no tomorrow. When the sun rose the next day, Adam knew that he had been given a second chance.[8] When he discovered the power of repentance, he sang Psalm 92 for the Sabbath day.[9]

Every Friday night and Saturday morning, Jews say this psalm, which extols God and discusses evildoing and righteousness. This expresses what Adam learned—that repentance is in line with the Sabbath's true purpose.

Each week, the Sabbath reminds us of our spiritual purpose and strengthens us to live as we should. When we do the wrong things, the special closeness to God that we feel on the Sabbath encourages us to repent for our misdeeds and get back on the right spiritual track.

The connection between repentance and the Sabbath is also reflected in their spellings. The Hebrew word for Sabbath (*Shabbat*) consists of the Hebrew letters *shin, bet,* and *tuv*. These letters also spell *tashuv*, which means returning to where we are supposed to be via repentance. These same letters also spell *boshet*, or "embarrassment." When we do things that we shouldn't, we feel embarrassed. If we use the closeness to God and the spirituality that we sense on the Sabbath to help us repent, we remove our embarrassment by improving our behavior and returning to our Source.

The Straight Way. The Sabbath psalm concludes that God "is straight, my Rock, and there is no crookedness in Him." This means that He has run the world in the most straightforward way possible since Adam sinned. When we feel that God is absent and we can't see meaning or purpose in life, this psalm reminds us that He guides history.

Every seventh day, we are reminded that our purpose is to implement the Almighty's spiritual plan for the world. This "straight" path leads us to where we need to be, even though we won't see how until the Messiah comes. We are continually moving toward the Messianic era, which should have begun on the first Sabbath.[10]

Day of Rest

Every Seven Days. The Jews gave the world the idea of a weekly day of rest. Two modern societies tried to institute a day of rest every five[11] or ten days,[12] but both experiments were utter failures. It is thanks to the Jews that Westerners, Christians the world over, and many Moslems take for granted that people need a day of rest at least every seven days.

Seventh Day on the Seventh Day. To differentiate themselves from us, Christians moved the Biblical day of rest to the first day of the week, Moslems to the sixth day. Jews continue to observe the Sabbath on the seventh day of the week.

Three-Way Rejuvenation. Although the Sabbath's essence is spiritual rejuvenation, when we rejuvenate ourselves spiritually we also enjoy emotional and physical rejuvenation. As it says, "Six days you shall do all your work and do all of your constructive activity [*melacha*], and the seventh day is a Sabbath to the Lord your God."[13] If we can't work, write, do household chores, drive a car, or use the telephone, computer, and appliances, and we eat three leisurely meals with good food, spend time with our families, pray, and learn Torah, we become "reJewvenated."

What Is *Melacha*? It is a common misconception that turning on lights on the Sabbath is forbidden because it once took a great effort to light a fire. Some people think that since we can now have light with the flick of a switch, there is no reason to observe this prohibition.

The prohibition against *melacha* forbids doing any of the 39 constructive activities (*melachot*) associated with building the Tabernacle that the Jews made after receiving the Torah.[14] This connection between the Sabbath and the 39 Sanctuary-related creative acts is alluded to when God tells the Israelites to build Him a Sanctuary, yet to keep the Sabbath (meaning to refrain from performing even Sanctuary-building acts on the holy Sabbath).[15] (While the 39 *melachot* are forbidden by the Torah, Jewish prophets later added to these prohibitions additional acts that violate the spirit of the law.)

While modern technology was not around then, its principles were, and many activities that control or manipulate modern-day inventions are forbidden on the Sabbath due to similarity of principles. Thus, transferring fire, causing combustion, and completing a circuit are a few of the activities forbidden on the Sabbath, regardless of how little effort is involved.

Some forbidden activities require a lot of work, while others require very little. If the activity involves the same principles as the 39 *melachot*, it is forbidden on the Sabbath.

Putting Creativity and Productivity in Their Place. Sabbath-observers are continually reminded that, as wonderful as it is to be creative and productive, we shouldn't think that we are Masters of the world. One day a week, observant Jews don't travel, watch television, listen to the radio, or use telephones, computers, video games, or electric and battery-operated appliances. Lights and air conditioning may be operated by timers, or may be turned on before the Sabbath and left on. Jews don't feel compelled to check e-mail or respond to telephone calls.[16] They defer shopping and doing laundry and chores. Their businesses and offices are closed, and all work-related activities are put on hold—psychologically and practically—during the Sabbath. They even avoid conversing about mundane topics and business. Instead, they can immerse themselves in spirituality and enjoy quality time with their families, guests, and friends.

Many Jews initially think that observing the Sabbath's restrictions must be terrible. Once they try observing all or part of a Sabbath, together with its wonderful food, singing, quality family time, and Torah learning, they usually love the serenity and fulfillment that it brings! They then wonder why they didn't try it sooner![17]

Notes

1. Genesis 2:1-3. These verses actually appear before the episode in the Garden of Eden, yet they occurred after the first couple sinned. The Torah sometimes "backtracks" to flesh out prior episodes. This reflects a concept that the events in the Five Books of Moses are not always written in chronological order. Sometimes, we are meant to learn more by the way it connects ideas that are presented out of order.

2. This is implied in God's name *Sha-dai*, which is an acronym for the Hebrew words, "*She'mar l'olamo dai*"—He said to the physical universe, "Enough. If you increase any more, people will not be able to find Me behind the material world."

3. Genesis 2:1.

4. Ohr Hachaim on Genesis 2:1.

5. Historically, Jews ate fish and/or meat on the Sabbath, although one who doesn't like meat may eat any kosher food that makes the Sabbath day special.

6. Provided the couple is allowed to be intimate according to Jewish law, such intimacy draws the Divine Presence into their home.

7. *Genesis Rabbah* 19:5 says that Eve gave Adam squeezed grapes, which were the forbidden fruit, on Friday. The forbidden fruit would have been permitted to him had he waited only a few hours until the Sabbath began. Jews rectify Adam's sin every Friday night by using the fruit with which he sinned to bring us closer to God. This is known as making *kiddush* (sanctification). The verses recited during *kiddush* affirm God as Creator of the world and remind us to honor and guard the Sabbath by not doing forbidden acts on this holy day.

8. *Genesis Rabbah* 11:2.

9. *Genesis Rabbah* 22. Adam discovered the power of confession and repentance from his son Cain. God pardoned Cain after Cain murdered his brother Abel. When Adam heard this, he said Psalm 92. This Midrash makes a play on the Hebrew word *"l'hodot"* in Psalm 92, usually translated as, "to thank." Most translations say, "It is good to give thanks to the Lord." However, *"l'hodot"* can also mean "to confess." Thus, Adam said, "It is good to confess to the Lord and to sing to Your Name on high."

10. Had Adam not eaten the forbidden fruit on the day that he was created, he would have fulfilled the purpose of Creation, and the Messianic era would have started that evening. The Talmud (*Shabbat* 118b) says, "If the Jewish people observe two Sabbaths, they will be immediately redeemed." They will need the first Sabbath to stop trying to control their physical surroundings and let go of their material preoccupations. They can then fully embrace the soul of the second Sabbath by immersing themselves in spiritual truth and reality.

11. In 1929, the Communists in the Soviet Union tried to abolish religion by instituting a five-day continuous workweek with 80% of the people working on any given day and 20% having the day off. After eleven years of

disappointing production and epidemic work irresponsibility, Stalin reinstituted the seven-day week.

12. The humanistic French Revolution tried to substitute an Age of Reason to replace regressive religious superstitions. They devised a secular, "rational" week of ten days that was approved by the ruling Convention in October 1793. Every tenth day, the "decadi," was reserved for rest and celebration of various natural objects and abstract ideas. When the First Republic of France fell apart in 1805, the French people went back to a seven-day week.

13. Exodus 20:9.

14. Mishnah *Shabbat* 7:2 lists these 39 categories as sowing, plowing, reaping, binding sheaves, threshing, winnowing, selecting something desirable by taking away what is not wanted, grinding, sifting, kneading, baking, shearing wool, laundering, beating wool, dyeing, spinning wool, weaving, making loops when weaving wool, weaving threads, separating threads, tying a knot, untying a knot, sewing two stitches, tearing, trapping an animal, slaughtering an animal, flaying an animal, salting meat, curing a hide, scraping a hide, cutting up a hide, writing, erasing two letters, building, tearing a building down, extinguishing a fire, lighting a fire, putting on a final touch in making something usable, taking an object from a private domain to a public area or transporting an object in the public domain.

15. *Shabbos* 97b on Exodus 35:1-19.

16. It is permitted to violate all of the laws of the Sabbath, such as using a telephone or driving a car, to save someone's life.

17. For a fuller explanation and description of how the Sabbath is observed, see jewfaq.org/Shabbat.

The Tree of Life

The beautiful world that the Creator made was meant to usher in the Messianic era with the first Sabbath, just a few hours after Adam's and Eve's creation. Instead of obeying God and fulfilling this divine plan, humanity would now have to follow a much longer alternative track to bringing the world to spiritual perfection.

Genesis tells us what happened in the Garden of Eden after God informed Adam and Eve about His new plan for them. He said to the angels,

> *"Truly, the man has become like one of us, knowing good and evil. And now, lest he send forth his hand and take also from the Tree of Life and eat, and live forever."*
>
> *And the Lord God sent him from the Garden of Eden to work the earth from where he was taken. And He chased out the man, and He positioned from the east of the Garden of Eden the angels and the flame of an ever-turning sword to guard the way to the Tree of Life."*[1]

This passage raises so many questions; among them, why was God concerned that man would eat of the Tree of Life only after he knew good and evil? Why didn't He simply get rid of the Tree of Life if He didn't want people eating from it? Why did the Almighty assign angels—whatever they are—to guard the Tree of Life?

Bringing Death into the World

We can unravel this enigmatic passage by tracing Adam and Eve's metamorphosis in the Garden of Eden. As we discussed, they initially knew only truth. Their souls totally controlled their bodies, so their bodies weren't vulnerable to nature, death, and decay. At that time, only goodness and blessing existed. When Adam and Eve sinned, they partly disconnected their souls from their bodies.

As was mentioned earlier, the physical world and nature were immortal only when totally suffused by spirituality, which is part of

God and never dies or decays. Death, disease, and destruction only became possible because people violated the divine will and thereby severed the perfect bond through which spirituality was supposed to have infused the physical world. The Tree of Life represents our perfect fulfillment of God's will. When we act in concert with His will, we can control nature.

What benefit was there to death's entering the world?

Knowing that we will die some day makes us want to achieve some form of immortality on Earth. That knowledge motivates us to work hard and raise children to ensure that we will be remembered. Some of the ways that we strive for immortality can be in concert with the divine plan for the world, while others may not be. For example, some people exploit others, amass money unethically, or achieve notoriety for their immoral behavior. They become famous, powerful, and/or rich, but often for doing things that are spiritually destructive. Unfortunately, secular books and the media tend to celebrate such people and pay scant attention to those who bring the world closer to its intended goal.

Two Routes to Immortality

God didn't want people to take the easy route to immortality by eating from the Tree of Life after eating of the Tree of Knowledge of Good and Evil, but rather by perfecting themselves spiritually. Were people to live forever without striving for moral perfection, corrupt people would always control the world and subvert the divine plan for it.

There is an idea that God *wanted* Adam to eat of the Tree of Knowledge of Good and Evil, but only after first eating from the Tree of Life.[2] Adam needed to first internalize how to properly use knowledge before eating the fruit of that tree. He could have done so by not eating the fruit of the Tree of Knowledge until God allowed it. Had Adam eaten of the Tree of Life by obeying God, God would have allowed him to eat from the Tree of Knowledge after the first Sabbath began. Eating the fruit then would not have had negative consequences.

The Tree of Life is a metaphor for Torah (divine) knowledge, which expresses the divine will for us. The only way to really appreciate and enjoy the intellectual, physical, and emotional pleasures of life is by first understanding how God wants us to partake of the physical world.

Unfortunately, Adam thought that he knew more than his heavenly Parent did. He decided to experience life and knowledge first, then learn God's will for him.[3] This rationalization led to a fatal error that we also make.[4] Like Adam, once we taste forbidden fruit, we internalize the wrong desires and can be readily misled.

We can now understand what happened after Adam sinned. If the Tree of Life in the Garden were an easy road to immortality, it would have been disastrous for Adam to live forever after being corrupted. One sin would have led to another, and he would have had no motivation to improve either himself or the world. So God put angels—spiritual beings who only do their Creator's will—near the Tree of Life to prevent people from becoming immortal in the wrong way.

We must journey on the road less traveled and actualize ourselves by using the Torah's directives to overcome moral struggles and challenges, not take the easy way out. As we morally perfect the world and ourselves, the Tree of Life will once again be accessible to us.[5]

Human Logic vs. Divine Wisdom

Another explanation of the two trees in the Garden suggests that the Tree of Knowledge represents human logic, while the Tree of Life represents divine wisdom. God, not man, should determine what is truly good or evil. He wants us to use our intelligence, but in ways that He defines as good and true. The "snake" (negative inclination) in us tells us to ignore His directives. This inclination convinces us that we are smart enough to chart our own life paths and define for ourselves what is right and wrong.

The Twirling, Fiery Sword

Why is man's path to the Tree of Life barred with a twirling, fiery sword? The twirling causes us to sometimes see bright fire, sometimes not. That symbolizes our inconstant focus on God.[6] Sometimes we see clearly that there is a Creator who is constantly overseeing the world and designing the events of our lives with a purpose in mind. We fully believe at times that we should follow His will for us. At other times, we disobey Him because we don't believe that He is always near, caring, or keeping our best interests in mind. Our desires blind us to how we should really be living moment by moment, and we don't see the Tree of Life. It is up to us to remove those barriers that get in the way of our living fully with a consciousness of the Master of the World and His will for us. We can only return to Paradise when we continually want a relationship with the One Above and do what He wants of us. If the Jewish people would all do this, the world would be spiritually perfected and all goodness would be ours.

Alternate Route to Paradise

When Adam and Eve missed their opportunity to perfect the world, they consigned us to an "alternative track." That means that we have a limited amount of time within which to bring the world to spiritual perfection. If we don't succeed in our mission by the end of the time divinely allotted, God will bring the Messianic era anyway.[7]

Implications for Us

We tend to think that nature and scientific laws run the world. For example, if someone gets sick, we turn to doctors or technology to heal us, thinking they have the ultimate power to cure us. While we should avail ourselves of the best that medicine and technology have to offer, we also should remember that they are only God's agents. The One who created nature also controls how it operates.

Research has shown that religious involvement and prayer both have beneficial effects on one's health. Religious people recover more quickly from major surgery and have less disease, depression, drug and alcohol use, and incidence of suicide than others.[8]

It is noteworthy that the residents of Bnai Brak, a town almost exclusively of observant Jews near Tel Aviv, Israel, have the longest life expectancy of any group of Israelis. They are also one of the poorest cities in Israel, whose residents eat poor diets and exercise little.[9] Their longevity has no scientific explanation. Could it be that their observance of Torah results in God's overriding the rules of nature for them?

"Fully three-quarters of the 300 studies to date of the relationship between religious belief and health have shown a positive correlation. Various studies have shown that religious belief and regular attendance at religious services is associated with reduced doctors visits, a reduced incidence of certain forms of cancer and heart disease, and lower post-operative mortality and quicker rates of recovery."[10]

Studies have even shown that sick or hospitalized people who pray or who are prayed for, even when they don't know that others are praying for them, fare better than others in their circumstances who try to recover without prayers.[11] Countless people are alive today as a result of people begging the Source of Life to intervene, and His giving very ill patients a new lease on life.

People sometimes scoff at the idea that our lives would be better if we lived according to God's will. If He created and controls disease, genes, and scientific laws, He can change the way nature functions and make it more favorable to us when we accomplish His purposes by changing ourselves and connecting to Him.

Notes

1. Genesis 3:22-24.
2. Rabbi Motty Berger expressed this idea in a 1990s lecture at Aish HaTorah in Jerusalem. He quoted the verse in Genesis 2:16, "From *every tree* in the Garden you *should* eat, but of the Tree of Knowledge of Good and Evil you must not eat, for on the day you eat of it, you will die." Since the Almighty doesn't lie, He wanted Adam to eat freely from every tree in the Garden, including the Trees of Life and Knowledge of Good and Evil. Once Adam would have eaten from the Tree of Life—which metaphorically meant obeying one divine command—it would have been safe for him to then eat of the Tree of Knowledge.
3. When the Jews received the Torah at Mount Sinai, they spiritually rectified Adam's sin by saying, "We will do and we will hear" (Exodus 24:7), meaning, "We will do what God wants us to do, then we will hear His reasons for wanting us to do so." Adam decided that his logic was better than God's, and so he acted on the basis of his own logic. The Israelites decided to accept the Almighty's reasoning on faith and follow His commands, rather than deciding to obey Him only if His ideas made sense to them. Only after pledging obedience did they ask to understand the deeper meanings of the commandments.
4. The Law of Unintended Consequences is an idea that almost all human actions have at least one unintended consequence. Many times, these are more devastating than we could possibly foresee. For example, the Plague of Justinian in 541–542 CE was a pandemic of bubonic plague that probably originated in Ethiopia or Egypt. The huge city of Constantinople imported massive amounts of grain, mostly from Egypt, to feed its citizens. That seemed like a perfectly reasonable thing to do. But those grain ships probably harbored rats whose fleas carried bubonic plague. The massive public granaries then nurtured the rat and flea population. At its peak, the plague killed 5,000 people daily in Constantinople and ultimately destroyed up to a quarter of the people in the eastern Mediterranean. These material negative consequences parallel the spiritual ones when we act as if we know better than God what's best. We don't have His infinite wisdom and can easily overlook, or be unaware of, the repercussions of where our well-intended actions may lead.
5. After the Messiah comes, there will be a resurrection of the dead. From then on, there will be some form of immortality for the united body with its soul.
6. *Netivot Shalom* on this verse.
7. *Avodah Zarah* 9a states that this world as we know it will only exist for six thousand years: "Tanna Devey Eliyahu taught: The world is to exist 6,000 years—the first 2,000 are to be "void" [of Torah], the next 2,000 are the period of the Torah [from Abraham until the completion of the Mishna], and the following 2,000 are the period of the Messiah [i.e., the Messianic Age could start any time during this period]." We are now in the year 5768. This is why, with the many amazing events that have occurred in recent years (such as the return of large numbers of Jews to Israel, the renewed

productivity of the land, and the return of many secular Jews to observance), there is a widespread belief that we are now living in the era of the "footsteps of the Messiah."

8. See, for example, D. A. Matthews, et al., "Religious commitment and health status: A review of the research and implications for family medicine." *Archives of Family Medicine* (7)2, Mar-Apr 1998, pp. 118-124. These authors analyzed 68 research studies, of which 60 studies showed positive effects of religious involvement on health. See also Harold Koenig's extensive discussion of research on the positive effects of religion on mental and physical health in "Is Prayer Good for Your Health? A Critique of the Scientific Research." Heritage Foundation. Lecture #816, December 22, 2003, Washington, D.C. More than 1,000 research and review articles were published addressing this topic in 2000 to 2002. Seventy percent of the studies showed a positive effect of religious involvement on physical and mental health.

9. Rosenblum, Jonathan. "L'chaim in B'nai Brak," http://www.torah.org/features/spirfocus/bnaibrak.html

10. *Ibid.*

11. Byrd, Randolph, "Positive therapeutic effects of intercessory prayer in a coronary care unit population." *Southern Medical Journal* (81)7, July 1988, pp. 826-829. Dr. Byrd was a heart specialist at the San Francisco General Hospital, where he studied 393 patients who were admitted to the hospital's Cardiac Intensive-Care Unit. He randomly assigned them to a group that was prayed for and a second group that was not prayed for. He found that those who were prayed for were much less likely to develop congestive heart failure and pulmonary edema; they were five times less likely to require antibiotics; significantly fewer needed to be put on ventilators and receive artificial respiration; and significantly fewer developed pneumonia or had cardiac arrests.

Pleasure

According to one opinion in the Talmud, the Tree of Knowledge was a grapevine.[1] Wine epitomizes the material world. Used judiciously, it can lift our spirits and add to our happiness. Misused, it can lead to our downfall.

God wants us to experience every permitted pleasure in this world. In fact, the Talmud says that when a person dies and his soul goes to the next world, he must account for every permitted pleasure he refrained from enjoying while he was alive.[2] When the Temples stood, someone who vowed to abstain from wine for 30 days (known as a Nazirite) had to bring a sin offering for foregoing the pleasure of drinking wine for this short time.

The purpose of legitimate pleasures is for us to use them to serve our Creator. Before eating a delicious fruit, we can think, "God loves me so much that He created beautiful, fragrant, tasty, and nourishing food to sustain me." We then say a blessing over the fruit, acknowledging God as its Creator. When we eat it, we feel connected to the Giver of that pleasure. When we finish eating, after the immediate pleasure is over, we thank Him for the nourishment, satiety, and/or pleasure that we got.

Some people are wise to abstain from permitted pleasures they will not use properly. For example, an alcoholic should not have even a small amount of wine or liquor. Some pleasures also can't be used to serve God. For example, the Torah lists a variety of forbidden sexual relationships, as well as foods that Jews are forbidden to eat. The Almighty made these off-limits because indulging in them cannot be spiritually productive. Experiencing the many permitted pleasures of this world is an integral part of our service to our Creator, provided we do it in ways that sanctify ourselves and the world around us.

Rabbi Hirsch Takes a Hike

When Rabbi Shimshon Raphael Hirsch (a 19th-century German rabbi and famous Torah commentator) was an old man, his students were shocked to see him heading for the Alps. "Why is the Rabbi taking time from studying Torah to go hiking?" they asked.

"I'm approaching the end of my life," he responded, "and it won't be long before my soul goes to the next world. When I get there, the Almighty will ask me, 'So, Shimshon, what do you think of My Alps?' What will I say if I never saw the beautiful mountains that He put here for us to enjoy?"

The Torah teaches that everything can serve a spiritual purpose, provided we know when and how to indulge, what and when to reject. We are supposed to live balanced lives, being neither ascetics nor hedonists. Following the Torah helps us stay emotionally and physically healthy and balanced so we can optimally serve our Creator.

Judaism rejects the idea that the body is the enemy of the soul. Living by the Torah is supposed to be a "way of pleasantness."[3] By foregoing forbidden pleasures—and properly appreciating permitted ones—we can fully enjoy eating, drinking, and marital relations. If we view every permitted pleasure as a warm embrace from our Creator, and feel how much He loves us through these gifts, we can relate to the physical world with a sense of fullness and joy. By refraining from forms of pleasure that are physically or spiritually damaging, we can appreciate even more the true worth of that which is permitted.

Implications for Us

In the 1970s, a Russian teenager left his country and settled in the United States. He immediately enrolled in a yeshiva, a school where Jewish boys study Judaism. He was soon living as an observant Jew.

A few months later, someone asked him, "Boris, when you lived in the USSR, you could do exactly as you pleased. You ate whatever food there was without worrying if it was kosher or not. You played sports or swam on Saturdays and went out with friends on Friday nights. You could drink, date, talk, and dress any way that you liked. Why did you give it all up and become observant?"

With a twinkle in his eye, Boris replied, "When I lived in a world without a Creator, everything was permitted, but none of it had meaning. Now that I know that the world has a Creator, I am limited in what I can do, but it all has meaning."[4]

When everything is permitted, nothing has true value. When all physical pleasure is forbidden, only a part of us can connect to our Creator. God put us in a material world filled with pleasures and told us how to use them in a balanced way so that we will feel close to the One who put everything here with a purpose and so that we will enjoy meaningful lives.

Notes

1. *Sanhedrin* 70a.
2. Yerushalmi, *Kiddushin* 4:12.
3. Proverbs 3:17.
4. Heard from Rabbi Moshe Eisenman at a Shabbat dinner in New York City in 1990.

Adam's and Eve's Burials

Jewish tradition says that Adam and Eve were buried in the Cave of Machpelah in the Israeli city of Hevron (Hebron).[1] The Cave is a holy site for Jews,[2] because of the Jewish patriarchs and matriarchs laid to rest there. Jews have prayed there since Biblical times due to its sanctity.

The word *Hevron* means "attached." *Hevron* is so named because it joins this world to the next.[3] When people have near-death experiences, they often report having traveled through a tunnel to a source of light, and/or having met their deceased relatives in that world.[4] The Zohar (the main book of Jewish mysticism) teaches that souls leave this world through the cave where Adam and Eve are interred—the Cave of Machpelah—regardless of where our bodies are laid to rest.[5] That same description in the Zohar mentions that when Abraham went to inspect the Cave of Machpelah before buying it as a burial place for his wife Sarah, he saw "a door open to Paradise," and "he saw a shining light that lit up the cave." Jewish tradition also says that each person sees the Divine Presence just before dying.[6] It is interesting how consistent our ancient traditions are with what is described by many people who have had near-death experiences.

When God punished the first couple, He told Adam, "From dust you are, and unto dust you shall return."[7] Since a corpse housed a soul during its sojourn on earth, it must be accorded respect after death through burial. Jews are not allowed to be cremated, embalmed, or "viewed" at a funeral; rather, they are buried in the earth as soon as possible after death.[8]

When the body dies, the soul separates from it and eventually goes to the next world. There it is asked, "Were you honest in business? Did you try to have children? Did you partake of every permitted pleasure that was available to you?" Souls of Jews are also asked if they hoped every day that the Messiah would arrive and that ultimate redemption would occur. The souls of Jewish men are additionally asked if they set aside time to study Torah every day.[9]

Every soul then goes through a "life review" where it sees all of its deeds and their effects. The soul is then judged and goes to a place of punishment for the sins it committed. Meanwhile, the body decomposes in the earth. There, it awaits future reconstruction when its purified soul will re-enter it in the Messianic era.[10]

When the soul's term of punishment ends,[11] it goes to the place of eternal spiritual reward. There the soul enjoys the fruits of the person's spiritual efforts and moral accomplishments. It has an intimate closeness with God that is proportional to how much the person attempted to do His will while he or she was alive. The pleasure of each moment of such intimacy is indescribable.[12]

Implications for Us

We frequently fill out forms that ask, "Who are you? What is your occupation? What is your permanent address?" We should think about how we will answer these questions when our Creator confronts us with them: Who were we? What eternal truths did we live for? How did we occupy our time? Did we leave the world a more moral, harmonious, and truthful place? Did we live a truly meaningful life from God's point of view?

By occasionally contemplating what our true "permanent address" will be, we can live fully with few regrets about who we were and how we spent our time and energy.

Notes

1. See *Pirkei d'Rabbi Eliezer,* 20, and *Zohar Chadash Ruth,* 79. This site is sometimes called the "Tomb of the Patriarchs" because Abraham, Isaac, Jacob, and their wives are buried there. The purchase of *Maarat HaMachpelah* (the Double Cave) and the surrounding field by Abraham is recorded for posterity in Genesis 23. More than two millennia later, Arabs built a mosque there and forbade Jews from entering the tombs of our forefathers and foremothers. In 1929, Arabs rioted against the Jews who lived in Hevron. Their vicious slaughter, raping of women, and pillaging left the city *Judenrein.* Today they claim that all of Hevron belongs to them and that Jews have no right to be there. The media insists that the hundreds of Jewish "settlers" who today live in this ancient Jewish inheritance have no legitimate reason to be there. More than 3,500 years of history tell us otherwise.

2. There are tens of thousands of Arabs in the area today, thanks to their 1929 riot against the Jews of Hevron. The Arabs confiscated the Jewish property and moved into their homes. They have also murdered and terrorized Jews who returned to lawfully owned Jewish buildings post-1967. The media informs audiences that this land rightfully belongs to the Arabs, ignoring thousands of years of Jewish connection to this holy place, Jewish purchase of the land and its buildings, and the Arab violence that wrested the area away from its rightful owners. Hevron is one of the four holiest cities in Israel for Jews.

3. *Zohar* 1:127a.

4. See, for example, the stories in Raymond Moody, *The Light Beyond*, New York, Bantam, 1988, and Ian Stevenson, *Children Who Remember Past Lives.* University Press of Virginia, 1987. Dr. Stevenson researched 2,000 cases of children who remembered past lives.

5. *Zohar* 1:127a. *Chessed L'Avraham*, Maayan 3, Nahar 13 says, "It is already well known that the cave of Machpelah in Hebron, which is the burial site of the Patriarchs, is the entranceway to the subterranean Garden of Eden. This is hinted to when Abraham buys the cave (Genesis 23:16). He paid money that was *'ovair la'socher'*—negotiable currency. These words are numerically equal to the phrase, *'orach l'gan'*—the path to the Garden—as well as equal to the numerical value of the word *'chatzer,'* meaning courtyard. This suggests that the cave is to the Garden of Eden what a courtyard is to a home."

6. *Pirkei d'Rabbi Eliezer* 34.

7. Genesis 3:19.

8. A soul is partly punished for the person's inappropriate physical indulgences by becoming disillusioned with the body and with the values that led to the wrong pursuits. This is called *chibut ha'kevver*, meaning "attachment to the grave." The soul is especially pained perceiving the decomposition of the body, its former home. Burial hastens the end of this punishment, by bringing closure to the soul's relationship to the body. It is

therefore merciful to the deceased to bury the body as soon after death as possible.

9.   *Shabbat* 31a.

10. *The Way of God* I:3:11.

11. A Jewish soul gets punished for no more than 12 months. That is why a surviving relative says *Kaddish*, a prayer that sanctifies God in the presence of a quorum of ten Jewish men, for 11 months. *Kaddish* helps the deceased's soul to be judged meritoriously for having left behind offspring who sanctify God's Name. *Kaddish* is never said for a full year so as not to make a public statement that someone was so evil that he or she required 12 months of punishment and purification in hell.

12. For a fuller discussion of the soul, the afterlife, reincarnation, and resurrection of the dead, see Lisa Aiken's book, *Why Me, God? A Jewish Guide to Coping with Suffering*. Northvale, NJ, Jason Aronson, 1996. See also Yaakov Astor, *Soul Searching*, Jerusalem, Targum, 2003.

Part III:
From Cain to Abraham

Cain and Abel

Adam's and Eve's sin set the stage for their son Cain to live as if the purpose of life were to acquire things, which in turn resulted in people's focus and *raison d'être* becoming irreparably distorted and materialistic.

> *And the man knew Chavah* [Eve] *his wife, and she conceived and gave birth to Cain,[1] and she said, "I have acquired a man from the Lord." And she continued to give birth to his brother, to Hevel, and he was a shepherd and Cain was a worker of the ground.[2]*

God gives parents divine inspiration when they name their children, and the Hebrew names a parent gives reflect a child's spiritual essence. Eve called her first son *Kayin* (Cain), meaning "acquisition," because she sensed that he would be materialistic. He did become a farmer, an occupation that in agrarian societies often focused on materialistic interests such as real estate, food production, and acquisitions. To produce more and more, some farmers used slaves, and most of the ancient world sank into idolatry to "guarantee" the success of their crops. Farmers were thus the first to worship the forces of nature and to be involved with slavery.[3]

On the other hand, Eve named Cain's brother *Hevel* (Abel), which means "nothingness." He became a shepherd concerned with his flock's wellbeing, but for whom the material world was not very important. She sensed that this son would be very spiritual, as were the later shepherds Moses and David.

Hevel's name also foreshadowed that his life would end prematurely and that he would come to nothingness:

> *And it was in the end of days, and Cain brought an offering to the Lord from the fruits of the earth. And Abel also brought from the firstborn of his sheep, and from their fat, and the Lord turned to Abel and to his offering. And to Cain and his offering He did not turn and Cain was very angry and his face fell. And the Lord said to Cain, "Why are you angry, and why did your face fall? Behold, if you do good, you will be lifted up, and if you don't do good, sin is crouching at your door, and its desire is for you, but you can rule over it."*
>
> *And Cain said to Abel his brother, and when they were in the field, Cain rose up against Abel and killed him.[4]*

Why didn't God accept Cain's offering yet accept Abel's? After all, it was Cain's idea to sacrifice; Abel only mimicked him.

Gratitude to the True Owner. To answer this question, we must understand the Jewish concept of sacrifices. The One Above does not need sacrifices. People offer sacrifices to concretize the belief that we own nothing material and our Creator owns everything. He loans us our bodies and lets us use the world to fulfill our soul's purpose. We not only own nothing, we even owe Him our very existence.

Our lack of truly owning anything is reflected by Biblical Hebrew's lack of possessive nouns. In Hebrew, we say that someone is "the master" of an object, or "this is to me," but there are no verbs that mean "to possess" or "to have."

When Cain sacrificed to God, he gave inferior produce instead of the best of what he had.[5] This suggests that he believed that what he had was his and he did not owe his Creator anything. Cain arrogantly relinquished the minimum necessary to curry self-serving favor with the Almighty.[6] He did not believe in offering to the true Owner what was rightfully His. This contrasted with Abel's giving the best of what he had in a humble display of gratitude.

Falling Prey to Materialism. That "sin was crouching at Cain's door" meant that the Almighty understood Cain's true feelings and knew that his intentions were not pure. God tried to educate Cain to improve himself so that he would master his negative impulses instead of falling prey to them. Rather than working on himself to become less materialistic, Cain chose to destroy his brother, whom he felt threatened his ability to acquire everything he wanted.[7]

The more materialistic we are, the more we view others as threats. This is because the more we value life according to what we have, the more we assume that others want what we want. We will be deprived of limited resources if others take what we desire. We then try to conquer and control others and squelch their ability to take.

Spirituality is Limitless. The more spiritually attuned we are, the more we see others as extensions of ourselves, and the more we sense our commonality with them. Since spirituality is limitless, we are never threatened by others having more spiritually. There is enough spirituality for everyone to have an unlimited amount without anyone having less as a result.

The text mentions that Cain said something to Abel, but it never tells us what was said. The Midrash[8] says that Cain told his brother that he (Cain) owned the earth, so Abel said that he (Abel) owned everything that was moveable! Each brother wanted as much materially as he could get. Instead of feeling that there were more than enough riches for both of them—after all, the entire world was at their disposal!—the brothers were self-centered and greedy. If one brother got, the other one felt deprived. When push came to shove, Cain settled the dispute by murdering Abel.

Implications for Us

This story says so much about human nature. Throughout history, people have been jealous of what others had. Countless wars have been fought and millions of people murdered simply to amass more and more land and belongings because people's desires for material things are insatiable. No matter how much we have, we tend to want more.

It is bad enough that we make ourselves miserable ("Cain's face fell") by thinking that we have less than our neighbor. We often add insult to injury by convincing ourselves that the other person is unworthy of what he has and that we deserve it more. Once we do that, it is easy to rationalize using any means necessary to restore what we crave to its rightful owner—us!

God's admonition to Cain to rise above his jealousy reminds us not to waste our energy fantasizing about what others have and designing ways to get it. Instead, we should realize that the One Above provides each of us with exactly what we need to fulfill our unique purposes in life. If we don't have the bank account, house, spouse, children, or luxuries that others have, perhaps we aren't meant to have them. If we are meant to have them, we will get them if we act morally and do what is necessary to achieve those goals. We should make reasonable and appropriate efforts to get what we think we need and develop ourselves spiritually so we can use our possessions properly. When it comes to material things, sometimes the best way to be happy is to be satisfied with basics, or with what we already have.

Notes
1. Rashi points out that this form of the Hebrew verb "knew" signifies that Adam had already "known" Eve before they sinned, while they were still at the pinnacle of their spiritual purity in the Garden of Eden. Cain had been conceived and was born there, at a time when intimate relations were always positive.
2. Genesis 4:1-2.
3. Munk, Elie. *The Call of the Torah.* New York, Feldheim, 1980, p.108.
4. Genesis 4:3-8.
5. Rashi cites the *Midrash Tanchuma* on this verse which says that Cain brought linseed, something of little value.
6. Cain's descendants eventually became idolaters. They adopted his attitude that sacrifices would get them more of what they wanted from the forces that ruled the world. These descendants then offered sacrifices to idols to get abundant rain, children, crops, and the like.
7. *Pirkei d'Rabbi Eliezer* 21.
8. *Genesis Rabbah* 22:7.

Anger

Cain's jealousy of his brother motivated him to commit the first murder. When the Almighty confronted him with the heinousness of his crime, Cain justified his behavior by saying, "Am I my brother's keeper?!"[1]

The most technologically advanced societies today are just as cavalier as Cain was with respect to anger and violence. Psychologists tell us that expressing anger is normal and healthy. We are barraged by desensitizing, graphic portrayals of anger and violence in books, in movies, and on television. We continually see society's supposed role models responding to frustration with outbursts of temper or rage. School and intra-family violence are shockingly frequent.

Ethics of the Fathers describes how four different types of people handle anger:

> *There are four types of temperaments. One who is quick to become angry and quick to calm down—his gain is outweighed by his loss. One who is slow to become angry and slow to calm down—his loss is outweighed by his gain. One who is slow to become angry and quick to calm down is pious. One who is quick to become angry and slow to calm down is wicked.*[2]

Rashi explained that someone who is quick to anger and slow to calm is wicked "because through the anger he will come to sin, as it is stated, 'Do not become angry and you will not sin.'"[3] Judaism does not take a benign view of getting angry nor of threatening violence. The Talmud even likens someone who tears his clothes and destroys his property in his fury to someone who worships idols.[4] Such a person acts as if there were no God running the world.

While it is normal to feel angry in certain circumstances, we often fuel that anger, then express it destructively. Our Heavenly Father continually puts us in challenging or frustrating situations that will allow us to grow past our emotional limitations. Yet He also gives us free will to shout, belittle, curse, insult or hit others, throw objects in anger—and worse.

Most circumstances that make us angry should be nothing more than frustrations and annoyances. We mostly get angry due to our egos. We get angry when we think that we deserved better or are entitled to things that we didn't get. Our expectations and attitudes shape our feelings more than reality does.

Not everyone gets angry waiting a long time at the cashier or getting stuck in a traffic jam. Not all parents react angrily when their children don't do what they're told to do—for the fifteenth time. While such situations might frustrate most of us, the intensity of our reactions depends on our expectations. If we see others as extensions of ourselves, and our experiences as divine tests, we will respond more calmly. If we prepare ourselves for long waits by bringing a novel to read or a checkbook to balance or a CD player to listen to, we are not so upset by unexpected delays. Instead of fuming when people are chronically late, we can arrive equally late, go places without them, or catch up on our reading or telephone calls while we wait. If we encounter traffic tie-ups somewhat regularly, we can plan to travel at a different time, avoid going to those places, take a detour, or use the time to listen to music, informative radio programs, or taped Torah lectures, or to bond with family or friends who are with us.

Judaism tells us that while we may not be able to control our initial feelings, we are responsible if we fuel them further. We have the power to choose a healthy response. If we believe that we must vent our anger or explode, we will be prisoners of our basest instincts. It is up to us to develop constructive responses that will help us cope with the negative impulses that can ambush us at any time.

Implications for Us

We sometimes think we would be happy if we could only remove frustrations and disappointments from our lives. Cain reminds us that happiness depends upon our learning to cope with not getting what we want, not by getting everything that we want. It is easy to blame other people and outside influences such as nature or circumstances beyond our control for upsetting us, yet we are the only ones who can control the intensity of our emotions and how we behave. We shouldn't wait for upsetting situations to occur, then magically hope to respond to them calmly. We will only deal with them better by anticipating those scenarios that frequently confront us and preparing for them well in advance.

Rather than expecting our bosses, co-workers, spouses, children, parents, and neighbors to change into the perfect people that we want them to be, we can remind ourselves that we can only change ourselves. The fact that we are in a hurry is no reason to expect that salespeople, drivers, co-workers, and our family will speed up, too. As a sign says, "Your lack of planning does not constitute an emergency on my part." Instead of centering the world around ourselves, we should plan better to fit in with how the world really operates.

Some people keep hoping that their spouses will stop doing annoying things and that their children will magically become obedient, easy to live with, and helpful. It is far more useful to change our expectations and learn better parenting and communication skills. By being realistic, choosing our battles, taking responsibility to fix our contribution to a conflict, and letting go of what's not so important, we can become better people.

Like Cain, we can live in our own world and expect others to give us everything we want. Or we can develop patience, humility, faith in God, and coping and communication skills as we master our negative impulses instead of being their slaves.

Living as if we are our brothers' keepers means respecting others. Our wants are no more (or less) important than those of others, so we should not hurt or exploit others to get what we want.

If we trust that God will give us what we need, we will be able to deal with almost any type of disappointment or difficulty. No matter the outcome, we can feel good about who we are in the process.

Notes
1.	Genesis 4:9.
2.	*Ethics of the Fathers* 5:14.
3.	*Berachot* 29b.
4.	*Shabbat* 105b.

Humanity's Moral Decline

After describing Abel's murder, the Torah traces the moral history of humanity by succinctly telling us who were the prominent men of each generation. The terseness of each description reflects the utter meaninglessness of their lives. They were like animals that lived, propagated, then disappeared off the face of the earth:

> *And Cain knew his wife, and she conceived and gave birth to Chanoch. And he* [Cain] *built a city and called the name of the city after the name of his son Chanoch. And Irad was born to Chanoch, and Irad gave birth to Mechuyael, and Mechuyael gave birth to Metushael, and Metushael gave birth to Lamech.*[1]

Their names allude to their inclinations. Cain (*Kayin*) means "material acquisition." Cain built and named a city for his son, *Chanoch* (Enoch), meaning "education," thereby educating his son that building physical structures instead of being a moral person was the essence of life.[2] *Irad*, meaning "wild ass," followed. His name symbolized the abandonment of self-discipline and spirituality. *Mechuyael* means "the one who erased God's Name." *Metushael* (Methusaleh) means "those who ask for God are dead." His son *Lemech* was the first man to practice polygamy, and his son *Yaval* built temples for idolatry.[3] The moral state of the world was so bad by then that *Metushael* and *Lemech* were the outstanding men of their generations!

People often wonder why Genesis rarely speaks about women during this time. They must have existed since men had wives with whom they had children!

One answer[4] is that, although women were born throughout the early generations, the Torah considers a man and his wife as one unit. It usually mentions only the more observable and "outwardly directed" member of each couple, which was the man. This is not to imply that women were considered unimportant; given the moral decadence of these early generations, women might feel relieved not to have been singled out!

Notice also that Genesis mentions only one man—the leader—of each generation, who epitomized what everyone else in his era stood for. Their names reflect how Adam and Eve's initial mistake led to an avalanche of moral failures that worsened in each generation.

Implications for Us

These stories should remind us that we are just as corruptible as these early generations were. Once a society accepts immoral behavior and attitudes as normal, they quickly become popular. Once wrongs are condoned as right, the fabric of society can disintegrate within a generation.

During the past few decades, American society first condoned, then encouraged, behaviors that were once condemned. The country that once promoted moral values to its citizens and to the world now espouses moral relativity. Prominent liberals preach that there is no right or wrong. Abstinence by unmarried people has been replaced by abortion on request and indiscriminate sex with "protection." Advocating rights without responsibility has resulted in moral chaos.

Americans are now paying the price of advocating the right to pleasure over the responsibility of ethics and morality. High-school and college students routinely party with alcohol and drugs as a way to have "fun." More than 8% of Americans abuse alcohol or are alcohol-dependent, and 55 million Americans binge drink at least once a month.[5] Nearly 8% use illicit drugs.[6] In 2004, an estimated 22.5 million Americans were classified as substance dependent or abusers.[7] Sadly, it is no longer unusual to find children as young as twelve using both alcohol and/or illicit drugs.

Self-centeredness has trumped moral responsibility and self-discipline: more than 10,000 people are killed every year by drunk drivers,[8] and more than 15,000 people are murdered every year[9] across the United States.

> People are better prepared to earn money than they are to be proper parents and spouses. This is reflected by the fact that at least one-third of American marriages end in divorce, and cohabiting couples have twice that dissolution rate.[10] Only 63% of American children now grow up in families with both of their biological parents, the lowest rate for any nation in the Western world.[11]

Families headed by a mother and father are not valued by society more than "alternative lifestyles" and unmarried couples living together. The overwhelming majority of black children are born to impoverished single mothers, without the benefit of having their fathers in their lives. More than 1,200,000 American babies are aborted every year,[12] and epidemics of every sexually transmitted disease plague the United States. Americans live in the most materially affluent society in the world, yet in the devastating chaos of having no moral compass.

Cain and his offspring remind us of societies' disastrous ends when they do not follow the basic moral principles that God gave humanity.[13] When people live by their own definitions of right and wrong, chaos and moral decline invariably follow. Rights must be given in the context of moral responsibilities. Advocating material comfort and sensual pleasure as ends in themselves inevitably leads to moral and spiritual oblivion.

Notes

1. Genesis 4:17-18.
2. Munk, Elie. *The Call of the Torah*. New York, Feldheim, 1980, p. 122. Rabbi Shimshon Rafael Hirsch says that Genesis 4:17 describes not only Cain's actions, but also his personality.
3. Rashi on 4:20, quoting a Midrash.
4. Gur Aryeh on the above verse.
5. In 2004, about 45%, or 55 million, of the 121 million Americans who reported drinking alcohol said they participated in binge drinking at least once in the 30 days prior to the survey. And 16.7 million, or 14%, said they were heavy drinkers. The highest prevalence of binge/heavy drinking was among young adults ages 18-25, peaking at 21 years of age (2004 National Survey on Drug Use and Health, Department of Health and Human Services, http://www.oas.samhsa.gov/nsduh.htm#NSDUHinfo). The number of American adults who abuse alcohol or are alcohol dependent rose from 13.8 million (7.41%) in 1991-1992 to 17.6 million (8.46%) in 2001-2002, according to results from the 2001-2002 National Epidemiologic Survey on Alcohol and Related Conditions (NESARC), a study directed by the National Institute on Alcohol Abuse and Alcoholism (NIAAA).
6. In 2004, an estimated 19.1 million Americans, or 7.9% of the population, ages 12 and older were current illicit drug users (2004 National Survey on Drug Use and Health, Department of Health and Human Services, http://www.oas.samhsa.gov/nsduh.htm#NSDUHinfo).
7. 2004 National Survey on Drug Use and Health, Department of Health and Human Services, http://www.oas.samhsa.gov/nsduh.htm#NSDUHinfo.
8. According to preliminary data from the National Highway Traffic Safety Administration (NHTSA), in 2006, 17,941 people were killed in alcohol-related car crashes—an average of one every half hour. These deaths constituted approximately 41% of the 43,300 total traffic fatalities. Drunk (those at or above an illegal BAC of .08) drivers were involved in 13,990 fatalities in 2006. Statistics provided by Mothers Against Drunk Driving website, http://madd.org.
9. There were 23,677,800 assaults, car thefts, murders, rapes, and drug offenses committed in the United States in the year 2000, according to the Seventh United Nations Survey of Crime Trends and Operations of Criminal Justice Systems, covering the period 1998-2000 (United Nations Office on Drugs and Crime, Centre for International Crime Prevention). In 2005, there were 16,692 murders in the United States (United States Uniform Crime Report, www.disastercenter.com/crime/uscrime.htm).
10. Jayson, Sharon. "Divorce Declining, But So Is Marriage." *USA Today*, July 18, 2005.
11. *The State of our Unions 2005*. The annual report, which analyzes Census and other data, is issued by the National Marriage Project at New Jersey's Rutgers University.

12. Statistics supplied by the Guttmacher Institute show that American women have had between 1,000,000 and 1,600,000 abortions every year since 1975. The numbers have stayed fairly stable at around 1,300,000 since 1997.

13. These Seven Noahide Principles include prohibitions against idolatry, sexual immorality, theft, murder, eating a limb from a live animal, and cursing God, plus the requirement to set up courts of law.

Exploitation vs. Nurturing

As the world's morality declined, Genesis tells us how polygamy began:

> *And Lemech took two wives to himself. The name of the first was Adah and the name of the second was Tzillah.*[1]

Lemech was the first man to marry two wives, and he exploited both of them. A Midrash says that he married Tzillah for sensual gratification and used her as an object for his pleasure. He married Adah only to have children and deprived her of companionship.[2]

Genesis then tells us where this kind of behavior leads:

> *And Adah gave birth to Yaval. He was the father of those who sit in a tent and tend cattle. And the name of his brother was Yuval. He was the father of all who take the harp and the pipes.*[3]

Using Talents To Ennoble

Adah had one son who was the first professional shepherd,[4] while the other was the first musician. Instead of using their professions to spiritually ennoble themselves and others, they used their animals and music, respectively, in idol worship.[5]

If a shepherd or farmer wishes to focus on spirituality, he can see that his care for animals or crops is but a fraction of the nurturing the Almighty gives us. The shepherd must provide food for his animals, protect them from predators and severe weather, and nurse them back to health when they are sick. Our Heavenly Shepherd continually does the same for us.

Music can be very spiritual, making us aware of God and a reality that transcends what we can see and touch. It can affect our souls by bypassing our minds and embracing our hearts. Moses and David shepherded flocks before they became shepherds of the Jewish people. David was also a gifted musician whose music helped inspire him when he wrote Psalms. Unfortunately, neither Yaval nor Yuval were interested in directing their talents to similar ends.

Despite her initial role as a pleasure machine for her husband, Tzillah also became a mother:

> *And Tzillah also gave birth to Tuval-Cain,* [the father of all those who] *sharpen and forge copper and iron. And the sister of Tuval-Cain was Naamah.*[6]

Tzillah's son made the world's first weapons. His name was Tuval-Cain because he refined Cain's handiwork.[7] Cain had only crude implements for murdering, while Tuval-Cain made very high-quality instruments for killing.

From Short-Term Pleasure to Self-Centered Taker

Genesis tells us about Tuval-Cain's parents so that we will know that when a parent sees life's purpose as short-term pleasure, self-centered takers like him inevitably result. Tuval-Cain internalized his father's desire to conquer others for pleasure and wanted to destroy those who got in his way. It was a logical step for him to then make weapons of destruction.

Until someone conceptualizes a certain idea, the idea may lie beyond people's imaginations. Once someone invents a technology or innovates an idea, humanity then continues where that person left off. Technology has always been a double-edged sword. Tuval-Cain opened a Pandora's box that gave tools of destruction to mankind.

Giving is God-like. Adah, whose role was to bear and nurture children, was a selfless giver. Since God is a total Giver, people who are giving are therefore more spiritual and like the Almighty than takers are. That is why her son was attracted to music. A child of spiritually attuned parents is likely to be similarly oriented.

Tzniut. Adah also developed her attribute of *tzniut*. This has no real synonym in English, although it is usually (poorly) translated as "modesty," a term that does not begin to capture its true meaning. The concept of *tzniut* focuses on acting with dignified humility while seeing God in oneself and in others. Adah valued her Godly essence, and this allowed her children to bring a spirituality into the world that could never be totally corrupted.

Tzniut is a virtue that parents pass on to their children. Even when children rebel against good, moral parents who have beautiful character traits, children cannot totally divest themselves of the values that tzniut confers. Once children live in a home where truth and spirituality are important and life's superficialities are not, the children cannot act as if they haven't seen that. This is why some people who appear outwardly irreligious and non-spiritual may have tremendous spiritual depth and sensitivity. They have often inherited tzniut from their ancestors.

Righteousness from Wickedness. Despite giving birth to a son who became anti-spiritual, Tzillah also gave birth to Naamah, who acted virtuously and later became Noah's wife.[8] This teaches that even when someone is born to a family where there are wicked people, everyone has free will to become righteous.

Implications for Us

It is popular for sociologists and psychologists to absolve people of personal responsibility for their misdeeds and to blame society or their families for their failings. The genealogies of Genesis teach us that even though one's society or parents can be corrupt, every adult can choose to make a moral break with his past, as did Adah, Naamah, and Enosh (mentioned as "walking with God" in Genesis 5:22). Our respect for the divine image in ourselves and others and a desire to live up to the divine purpose in the world would prevent most of the world's sorrows. Adopting those perspectives will affect not only us, but many generations to follow.

Notes

1. Genesis 4:19.
2. Rashi on Genesis 4:19. Roman men later adopted these same practices.
3. Genesis 4:20-21.
4. While Abel was a shepherd, his life was so short that he did not have a chance to make a livelihood from shepherding.
5. Rashi on the verse.
6. Genesis 4:22.
7. Rashi on Genesis 4:22.
8. *Ibid.*

The Value of Life

After Genesis tells us about some of Adam and Eve's descendants, there is an enigmatic passage in which Lemech boasts to his wives that he is a murderer:

> *And Lemech said to his wives Adah and Tzillah, "Listen to my voice, wives of Lemech, give ear to my words, for I have killed a man by my wounding, and a child by my blow. For it took seven generations for Cain to get revenge, and Lemech will be seventy-seven."*[1]

To understand what this means, we must revisit Cain after he killed his brother. There is an idea[2] that after punishing Cain, God dressed him in the same skin garment that He initially gave Adam. That garment had all of the world's animals patterned onto it to symbolize that humans have the same drives as animals. It was supposed to remind Cain, and before him Adam, not to follow his animalistic instincts, but to live up to his inner divinity. It was a constant reminder that we have animalistic urges so that we will spiritually elevate them, not indulge them.

Rashi[3] explains that Lemech was blind. Just prior to this incident, his son Tuval-Cain had taken Lemech out to hunt. Not realizing that Cain was walking in the forest, Tuval-Cain saw Cain's animal skin moving in the distance and mistook it for an animal. Tuval-Cain told his father to shoot an arrow, and Lemech did, thereby killing Cain.

Lemech was upset when he realized what happened. When he struck his hands together in grief, he accidentally killed his son Tuval-Cain.

Lack of Remorse

When his wives heard what he had done, they wanted to leave Lemech. Instead of regretting his terrible deed, he bragged to his wives in the above verses that nothing bad was likely to happen to him. He wasn't bothered for long about having snuffed out two lives; his only concern was that he not get punished.

He reasoned that it took seven generations before Cain was killed for deliberately murdering his brother. Surely it would take seven times longer for Lemech to get punished for manslaughter. He reassured his wives that there was no reason for them to leave him because there wouldn't be any untoward consequences of his act for the foreseeable future.

This story illustrates how terribly people's morality had declined just a few generations after God created humanity. Instead of trying to fix the world spiritually, Lemech and his generation only cared about whether life was pleasant for them.

Rashi informs us that Lemech's wives separated from him because of his lack of remorse, yet he insisted that they rejoin him. Lemech implicitly threatened that if he could kill others, he could kill them, too.

This illustrates how societal violence and exploitation of women are intertwined. Societies that are materialistic or hedonistic often end up being violent and exploiting those who are powerless.

A Midrash[4] says that Lemech's wives left him despite his reassurances and threats because they believed that a flood would soon wipe out any children that they might have with him. They understood that the world had become so evil that it was doomed. They refused to come back to Lemech, so they all went to Adam and asked him to judge their grievance.

Lemech complained, "My wives refuse to live with me. Tell them that they are wrong."

Adam responded, "Lemech is right."

The wives replied, "He's doomed. What is the point of bringing more children into the world with him if the world is also doomed?"

Adam told the women, "Even if the world is doomed, it's worthwhile bearing children." They knew that God would annihilate mankind with a flood if people stayed so wicked, yet He had not yet decreed that. As long as He was still allowing children to be born and was sustaining people, it showed that their lives were valuable.

Infinite Value of Life

Creating life has intrinsic value, and life has infinite value—regardless of how much pleasure one gets, or how productive one is—because we each have a divine image inside ourselves. Every person has a purpose here as long as he or she is alive.

The wives countered to Adam, "So why don't you practice what you preach? You've been separated from your wife for 130 years!"

According to the Midrash, Adam had left his wife once they were expelled from the Garden of Eden. He did this because he thought this was the best way to repent and rectify his sin.

Talking to Lemech's wives convinced Adam that embracing life, not divorcing himself from it, would allow him to truly fix his sin. After rebuking Lemech's wives for separating from their spouse, Adam followed his own advice and went back to his wife.

This is why the Torah immediately says after the incident with Lemech,

> *And Adam knew his wife again, and she gave birth to a son and called his name Shet (Seth), "For God appointed me another seed in place of Abel, for Cain killed him."*[5]

After Eve gave birth to *Shet*, we read,

> *Adam lived 130 years and he fathered in his image, like his form, and he called his name Shet.*[6]

The "his" in this sentence is ambiguous, and can also be read "in His image, like His form." Reading the sentence in the latter way means that God's image was more complete when Adam reunited with his wife than when the couple lived apart. Their reunion also resulted in a child who became the father of all humanity through *Shet*'s descendant, also named Lemech. This Lemech was Noah's father. In contrast with the Lemech who snuffed out lives, Noah's father was responsible for humanity's continuation.

Implications for Us

Lemech the bigamist mostly cared how much sensual pleasure he could get. Today, many people consider someone's life worthwhile only if they get pleasure or are productive.

Judaism teaches that as long as God gives someone life, that person's existence must serve a divine purpose. Rather than celebrating the virtues of euthanasia or certain forms of suicide, we should know that what is essential about life is far deeper than what meets the eye. Judaism has a code of medical ethics that teaches great respect for human life because every human being houses the divine image within him or her. If a person's body is deformed or they are very ill, mentally handicapped, or in pain, that does not justify snuffing out his or her life. If our Creator deems someone worthy of having life, who are we to decide that He made a mistake?

There are times when Jewish law does not require medical personnel to take extraordinary efforts to keep very ill people alive and the person is allowed to die as a disease takes its natural course. Yet doctors frequently refrain from giving terminally ill patients adequate painkillers and don't treat the depression of patients who say that they want to die. Most people who are seriously and/or terminally ill aren't depressed and don't want to die. When someone is medically ill and depressed and is adequately treated, it is rare that they don't want to live longer.[7]

We shouldn't convince ourselves when we aren't happy giving the time, effort, and money to care for someone who is seriously ill that that person's life is not worthwhile. Some people have been euthanized by doctors or relatives who felt that the ill person should be "put out of his misery," when there was no objective evidence that the ill person was actually suffering and/or the patient did not give his or her consent.[8]

A doctor once told a rabbi about a lonely old man in the hospital who was a "vegetable." He was being kept alive by a ventilator. Since the man had no known relatives, the doctor thought that he would do a good deed, have "mercy" on the patient, and disconnect the machine. That night, and each of the following two nights, the soul of the deceased man appeared to him in a dream. "I am summoning you to the Heavenly court. You deprived me of eleven days of life, during which time I was supposed to be cleansed of all my sins. Because you deprived me of that, I am suffering and incomplete here."[9]

According to the Torah, the doctor had committed murder.

As long as the Author of life hasn't yet taken someone from this world, we shouldn't think that we know better than He how to write the script. He will take the person's soul back at the right time. We don't have to help Him along.

Notes

1. Genesis 4:23.
2. From a taped lecture given by Rabbi Uziel Milevsky at Yeshivat Ohr Samayach, circa 1980s, on the Torah portion of *Bereishit*.
3. Rashi on 4:23.
4. *Genesis Rabbah* 23:4.
5. Genesis 4:25
6. Genesis 5:3.
7. See euthanasia.com. They quote a study published in the *Journal of the American Medical Association* that noted how few patients want to die if they are told about options to treat their pain and receive hospice care.
8. The study published in *JAMA* above also noted that only one-third of the doctors surveyed who performed euthanasia followed medically approved guidelines, and that in 15% of the cases the patient was never consulted. The patient was given a lethal dose of medication at the request of the family. Another example of the slippery euthanasia slope was reported by Clive Seale, a professor of sociology at Brunel University. He found that 1,930 deaths in Britain in 2004 were as a result of a doctor ending a patient's life without the patient's consent, a practice known as "non-voluntary euthanasia" or "mercy killing." Doctors performed another 936 euthanasias in Britain in 2004 with patient consent. They also hastened the deaths of 192,000 patients using medication to alleviate the patients' symptoms. Reported by Sarah Womack, "Doctors Involved in Eight Euthasia Deaths A Day." *London Telegraph*, January 18, 2006. According to lifeissues.org, Dutch doctors euthanize or help as many as 20,000 patients to die every year. Half of these patients did not ask to be killed.
9. In Astor, Yaakov, *Soul Searching*. Jerusalem, Targum, 2003, pp. 138-139.

Hitting Rock Bottom

As each successive generation came into the world, they corrupted themselves to a point where they became morally irredeemable. Cain committed the first murder, and Shet's son Enosh began practicing idolatry.[1] Enosh and his generation initially honored God's creations, while subsequent people invested those creations with divine powers, starting idolatry. Soon afterward, people forgot God.

Lemech began polygamy, and his son Tuval-Cain developed weapons of war. A mere ten generations after Adam's creation, men were using women as objects. Things were so bad that the Torah says:

> And it was when men began to multiply on the face of the earth, and daughters were born to them, and the sons of the gods [elohim] saw that the daughters of man were good and they took themselves wives from whatever they chose.[2]

One interpretation of the above verse is that the rulers[3] in Noah's time began a sordid practice that continued for thousands of years. When a woman looked especially beautiful—that is, on her way to the wedding canopy—the rulers (or their sons) raped her before she could consummate the marriage with her husband.[4]

The above verse says that these men not only abducted brides, they took wives from "whatever" they chose. This means that they had sex with married women, with men, with animals—with anything they lusted for.[5] The seeds of lust that Adam and Eve's sin brought into the world took root in the generations prior to the Flood.

God then responded to the total corruption of the once-pristine world that He created:

> My spirit will not rest with man forever inasmuch as he is flesh. And his days shall be 120 years. . . . And the Lord saw that the wickedness of man on earth was great and all

of the inclination of the thoughts of his heart were only evil all day.[6]

Implications for Us

We see how easy it is for people to go into a moral freefall once they stop believing in God and a divine plan for us. We continually have the choice of whose desires to follow—His or ours. If we stop viewing sensual pleasures as means of drawing us closer to our Creator, and don't direct our desires as He intends, we will inevitably view them as means for our own gratification. Once that happens, there is no limit to how far astray self-indulgence will take us.

Notes

1. Maimonides, *Mishnah Torah, Hilchot Avodat Kochavim* I:1-2. Rashi on Genesis 4:21 and Maimonides both explain the process by which idolatry began.
2. Genesis 6:1-2.
3. Besides referring to God, the word *elohim* can mean anyone in a position of authority, including leaders, judges, and even angels.
4. *Genesis Rabbah* 26:5. This was known as *ius primae noctis*. The Greeks did this when they ruled the Land of Israel during the 2nd century BCE. Judith, a Jewish woman, convinced them to stop this practice by beheading Holofernes, a Greek general.
5. *Genesis Rabbah* 26:5.
6. Genesis 6:3, 5.

Anthropomorphisms

As humanity had betrayed the purpose for which we were created, life no longer had a purpose. God created people only so that there would be recipients for all of the goodness that He wanted to give us. If mankind had no interest in a relationship with Him, there was no longer any reason to keep people alive. Genesis describes the Almighty's decision to bring a Flood:

> *And the Lord regretted having made man on the earth and He grieved in His heart. And the Lord said, "And I will blot out the man that I created from the face of the earth, from man to beast, to crawling things to the fowl of the heavens, because I regret that I made them."*[1]

This is one of many examples where the Torah says that God had a feeling such as regret, grief, or anger. These expressions of divine emotion are never meant literally. The Almighty has no physical form,[2] and human feelings do not apply to Him. The Torah only says that He has emotions so that we can have some way of understanding how He interacts with the world.

What, then, does the Torah mean by saying that the Almighty regretted His actions? He certainly knew when He created people that they would become corrupt!

The Midrash[3] answers this question by relating a conversation between a Gentile and Rabbi Joshua ben Korcha:

The Gentile asked, "Do you believe that God knows the future?"

"Yes," the Sage replied.

The non-Jew continued, "If so, why does the Torah say that God 'grieved in His heart'?"

The Sage replied, "Did you ever have a son?"

"Yes," the man responded.

"And what did you do when he was born?"

"I rejoiced and made others rejoice," the man answered.

"But didn't you know that he would die some day?" the Sage countered.

The man responded, "At the time of joy, let there be joy, and at a time of mourning, let one grieve."

"So, too, is it with God," the Sage explained. "Even though He knew that men would sin and need to be destroyed, He did not refrain from creating people for the sake of the righteous ones who would exist."

Since the Creator made a world so that He could give His goodness to people, which means having an intimate closeness with us, He "rejoiced" as long as people made themselves capable of receiving from Him.

Divine regret means that the Almighty was tremendously "disappointed" when people made it impossible for Him to give to them. As long as their actions allowed Him to give, He delighted in His world. When people forced Him to stop giving because of their terrible behavior, He "grieved."

Any loving parent can appreciate what this means. The parent wants nothing more than to give everything good to his or her child. The most painful state is for the child to reject the parent's desire for a relationship, and with it, the love and other gifts that the parent wants most to bestow.

Once humanity only valued the flesh and not the soul, God decided to give people 120 more years to repent. A world in which people had no desire to find or relate to their Creator would have no purpose. When that time passed and people showed no interest in finding Him, God had no choice but to destroy the world.

At that point, there is an idea that God "sat and mourned" for seven days before bringing the Great Flood.[4] His "crying" over the world that He was to destroy means that humanity forced Him to withhold His blessing because it would not be meaningful to them.[5] Nothing "pains" Him more than not being able to show us how much He loves us.

Implications for Us

The Talmud says that a person only sins because a "spirit of nonsense" enters him.[6] If we thought about God's pain, so to speak, when we reject Him, we would be more apt to live in ways that allow us to receive His goodness. If we truly loved the One who gives us life, we would think about how much He wants to give to us and how we need to live in order to make that possible. The greatest gift that we can give a loved one is to allow them to give us their deepest desire. God's greatest desire is to share His divine wisdom and love with us. When we allow Him to do this by making ourselves proper recipients of both, it not only gives our Creator spiritual pleasure, so to speak, it also benefits us immeasurably.

Notes
1. Genesis 6:6-7.
2. The Torah sometimes refers to God's body, such as His face, His strong arm, His back, and the like. God does not have any physical form. When God appeared to Abraham in Genesis 18:1, it means that Abraham totally sensed the intimacy of the Divine Presence. God was not physically nearer Abraham at that time than before; Abraham was simply able to sense His closeness more intensely.
3. Rashi on 6:6.
4. From a taped lecture on this Torah portion by Rabbi Yitzchok Kirzner, zt"l, at the Jewish Learning Exchange in Los Angeles.
5. The Maharal's explanation.
6. *Sotah* 3a.

The Generation of the Flood

While God is very loving, there is a point at which a parent's love needs to stop enabling a child's self-destruction. By Noah's era, continuing to give people life only gave them the chance to continue their spiritual destruction:

> . . . the earth became corrupt before God, and the earth was filled with violence. And God saw the earth, and behold, it was corrupt because all flesh had corrupted its way on the earth. And the Lord said to Noah, "The end of all flesh has come before Me because the world is full of violence through them, and behold I will destroy them with the earth. Make an ark of gopher wood . . . [and when I bring a flood to destroy everything on earth] you will come into the ark, and your sons, and your wife, and your daughters-in-law with them."[1]

The idea of divine punishment is often misunderstood. God doesn't punish people to take revenge for their disobedience. Rather, He becomes "disappointed" for our sake when we act improperly and we remove ourselves from the Source of truth, goodness, love, and eternal pleasure. Since He wants us to receive the utmost from Him, He punishes us so that we can fix the damage that we caused and learn to act differently the next time.

The Almighty resorted to destroying the world only after He had exhausted all other avenues for getting people back on the right spiritual track. One hundred and twenty years before the Flood, He instructed Noah to start building an ark. Like a loving Parent, He wanted to give humanity one last chance to act better. The Almighty hoped that people who saw Noah making an ark for so many years would be curious and ask him what he was doing.

When they asked Noah, he told passersby why God was bringing a Flood, and urged them to live properly so that it wouldn't come to pass. Yet no one listened to him.

Having free will means living with the consequences of our actions. We can't live as we please, then not suffer when we reap what we sow.

What did these people do that was so irreparably wicked that they had to die? Some commentators thought that it was worshipping idols or engaging in rampant sexual immorality.[2] Yet Rashi said that while sexual immorality and idolatry were widespread, "violence," which he defined as robbery, was the straw that broke the camel's back.

The commentators don't really disagree in their basic ideas, because all three reasons that they gave for the Flood have the same root.[3] People only steal if they don't believe that God gives each person exactly what they should have. He gives each of us different things so that each of us can achieve our unique spiritual goals. People from the time of Cain until Noah viewed the world as theirs instead of belonging to the Almighty, with people as its caretakers. As the world became filled with violence, people tried to acquire more and more material goods without accepting responsibility to use properly what they had.

We can only rightfully "own" anything after first acknowledging its Source, then using it to further His purposes. We do this by praying and by thanking God for giving us pleasures and material belongings that we use for His ends. We also acknowledge His ownership of the world by giving 10% of what we earn or acquire to charity.[4]

Idolatry and sexual immorality are rooted in the same egocentrism that leads to theft. People worship idols in an attempt to control natural forces to get more of what they want. Sexual immorality is enjoying hedonistic pleasure without relating it to a higher purpose.

The world loses its purpose and cannot go on once people see it as a place for self-gratification. People with this *raison d'être* usually end up hurting each other and themselves.

Implications for Us

The Jewish concept of prayer is that before asking God for what we want, we first judge ourselves. The word for prayer, *l'hitpallel*, means that we first consider how we have used what the Almighty has already given us, then consider how we will use what we want Him to provide.[5] We should only ask for what we want once we have resolved to take what He gives and use it in ways that will further His purposes. That makes it likely that whatever we get will be used in a spiritually constructive way.

Once we take just to have things, acquiring things cannot be purposeful, and can easily lead us to immoral or unethical behavior. Only by accepting that the true purpose of getting is to serve a higher purpose can we receive in ways that will help us become better people and make the world a better place.

Notes

1. Genesis 6:11-14, 18.
2. Some commentaries interpret "corruption of all flesh" to mean rampant sexual immorality. Even animals ("all flesh") mated with other species, something which was abnormal.
3. Attributed to commentator Avnei Nezer in a taped lecture by Rabbi Uziel Milevsky at Ohr Samayach Yeshiva in Jerusalem circa 1980s.
4. Jews are supposed to give to charities that either provide indigent Jews with their basic needs (such as food, clothing, shelter, and Jewish education) or support institutions that teach Torah. We are obligated to take care of other Jews before we donate to non-Jewish causes. Giving money to museums, cultural institutions, the arts, most hospitals, and the like, does not fulfill this obligation.
5. The root of the word is *pallal*, which means "to judge." *L'hitpallel* means "to judge oneself."

Noah and the New Order

After the Torah describes how corrupt people became, we would expect it to tell us that God punished these wicked people immediately. That didn't happen. Moreover, we might think that once the wicked were killed, righteous survivors would go on with their lives. That didn't happen, either. To understand why, let's see what Genesis says:

> *Noah was a righteous man, he was perfect in his generations; Noah walked with God.[1]*

That Noah "walked with God" despite being surrounded by corrupt people suggests that he was exceptionally righteous.[2] Others believe that he was only righteous relative to his generation. He had to do a lot more to become a truly giving person. This included spending 120 years building an ark and then taking care of the animals in it 24 hours a day for an entire year.

Noah's giving was the antidote to the universal taking in the world that God had to destroy. It was also how he fixed his personal failure of not doing enough to convince people to repent. It gave his family and himself the merit that saved them during the Flood. It also formed a new foundation for a world that was built on kindness and caring for others.

Fixing the World

Why did the people enter and exit the ark in different orders?

> *Noah, his sons, and his wife, and his sons' wives entered the ark.[3]*

When God commanded Noah to leave the ark after the Flood, He said,

Exit the ark, you, and your wife, and your sons, and your sons' wives . . . .[4]

These verses hint to the fact that men and women entered as separate groups, then exited as couples.[5] People and animals in the ark were forbidden to have sex, but it was permitted again once they left.[6] This abstinence rectified the sexual immorality that contributed to the destruction of the world.

After Noah and his family spent a year learning that the purpose of life was to give, not take, they were allowed to resume having marital relations and bring more children into the world. Man had to realize that sex should foster intimacy and giving and never be a means of self-indulgence that exploits others.

Implications for Us

Noah and the Flood remind us to share our resources, time, and talents with others and to see everything that we have as divine gifts to be properly used. We need to strike a balance between taking care of our material needs and sharing what we have with others.

Once we view our time, money, and talents as being ours, it is hard to part with them. If we instead view ourselves as asset managers for the Boss, it is much easier to give away what was not fully ours in the first place.

Judaism tells us not to be afraid that sharing will diminish what we have. The more we give,[7] the more God will give us so that we can give more. That is one of the most blessed ways of getting.

Notes

1. Genesis 6:9.
2. Some believe that Noah's main shortcoming was that he did not try harder to convince people to repent. It was not enough for him to be personally righteous; his spiritual level demanded that he do more to encourage others to be moral. See Elie Munk, *The Call of the Torah*, Jerusalem, Feldheim, 1980, pp. 155-156.
3. Genesis 7:7.
4. Genesis 8:16.
5. Rashi on Genesis 6:18, 8:16.
6. Sexual relations were also forbidden in the ark because it is improper to rejoice and enjoy oneself when there is widespread famine or a major calamity in one's vicinity. *Code of Jewish Law, Orach Chaim*, 240:12.
7. See Deuteronomy 14:22 and 15:8 for Biblical obligations to give charity. *The Code of Jewish Law, Yoreh Deah* (249:1) says, "If he has sufficient resources, he should give according to the need of the poor; if his resources do not extend to this, he should give up to one-fifth of his possessions for an ideal fulfillment of the *mitzvah*, one-tenth for a normal fulfillment. Less is an ungenerous fulfillment." Tosafot in *Taanit* 9a elaborates, "How can we deduce that [the Biblical obligation to tithe all one's produce] applies to loan interest, trading, and all other profits? From the word *'all.'* The verse could have stated 'your agricultural produce.' What is the significance of it saying 'all'? To include loan interest, trading, and all other profits."

    Judaism prohibits giving so much charity that one becomes impoverished and needs to take charity (*Ketuvot* 50a). We can give up to 20% of our assets and income to charity while we are alive. If we have heirs, we can leave up to one-third of our estate to charity when we die (*Kitzur Shulchan Aruch* 34:4; *Ketuvot* 67b).

Counting Days and Making Days Count

After humanity refused to improve itself, the Almighty brought the Great Flood:

And the rain was on the earth 40 days and 40 nights. . . . And the waters became very, very strong upon the earth and they covered all of the tall mountains that were under the heavens. . . . And all existence that was on the face of the earth was blotted out . . . and the waters stayed strong on the earth for 150 days.[1]

One of many facts that support the Torah's veracity is that many ancient people have told Flood stories.[2] While the details of the story vary from culture to culture, the fact that so many disparate groups spoke about a Great Flood implies that it really happened and was not made up by some Biblical author. Archaeological finds and geological changes found in the ancient near east[3] are also consistent with a Great Flood having occurred.

The Flood caused major world changes and was intended to start a new world. This is symbolized by its lasting 40 days. "Forty" in Jewish thought symbolizes a new creation. The Talmud says that a conceptus becomes a fetus at 40 days, Moses received the Torah on Mount Sinai in 40 days, and the Israelites stayed in the desert for 40 years. Jews immerse in a ritual bath that contains 40 measures of water, from which they emerge spiritually reborn. A flood for 40 days symbolizes that the world needed a total overhaul in which the old foundations were erased and a new one established.

Rather than simply being a torrent of rain, Jewish tradition says that the Flood was caused by boiling water that descended from above and that welled up from below.[4] It harmed the world's atmosphere, washed away topsoil, redistributed minerals, and made the air less wholesome than it was before. Nachmanides, a medieval rabbi and physician, said that the polluted air after the Flood and the change in climate after the dispersal in Babel were the reasons why people typically lived much shorter lives after the Flood than they did before it.[5]

God had blessed the early generations with enormous material prosperity and longevity, but they had misused both. He then shortened their lifespans to reflect their diminished spiritual actualization. If people had tried to perfect themselves and the world, living hundreds of years would have been good. Once people showed that they weren't interested in spiritual goals, the Almighty shortened their lives.

Implications for Us

One of the greatest gifts is time. When we read Genesis, we see clearly how our ancestors should have lived, yet they weren't certain of, or interested in, the moral choices that they should have made. God gave us a Torah so we won't squander precious years figuring out how to best lead our lives. We also have wise Sages to guide us so we can make the most of our time and use our resources to best advantage in this world.

If we study Torah and learn from our Sages' wisdom, then follow the life paths that they advocate, we can live meaningfully and not waste our time traveling paths that lead to no good.

Notes

1. Genesis 7:12, 20, 23, 24.
2. The Utnapishtim in the Epic of Gilgamesh, as well as the Aztecs, Incas, Mayans, Hopi Indians, Mesopotamian cultures such as the Sumerians and Akkadians, Matsya in the Hindu Puranas, Deucalion in Greek mythology, the Chinese, Japanese, and Polynesians all had stories of a "great flood" that devastated earlier civilizations. Wikipedia.org lists 23 civilizations that had such stories. According to Plato, a pre-flood civilization existed in a great island nation in the Atlantic Ocean called Atlantis, and in distant nations around the Mediterranean (including a pre-Greek and a pre-Egyptian civilizations) and in Asia. People had massive fleets, armies, and large cities. They knew how to write. There were divisions of labor (artisans, husbandmen, warriors, carpenters, rulers, shipbuilders, stone quarry workers, metal workers, merchants, and sailors). According to Plato, the island of Atlantis and the distant Mediterranean civilizations were completely destroyed and disappeared into the depths of the sea after a single day and night of violent earthquakes and floods.
3. For example, archaeologist Max Malloran concluded that the Genesis flood "was based on a real event which may have occurred in about 2900 B.C." M.E.L.Mallowan, "Noah's Flood Reconsidered," *Iraq* (26), 1964, pp 62-82.
4. Genesis *Rabbah* 33. See also *Sanhedrin* 108a.
5. Nachmanides' commentary on Genesis 5:4. He rejects Maimonides' opinion in the *Guide for the Perplexed* (II:47), which states that those individuals cited by the Torah as living remarkably long lives were exceptional and that most people lived lives of ordinary length.

The Rainbow

After Noah left the ark, he sacrificed some of the "clean" animals that he had brought into the ark. The Almighty then made a covenant with him:

> *And I establish My covenant with you, and I will not cut off all flesh any more with flood waters, and there will never again be a flood to destroy the earth. And God said, "This is the sign of the covenant that I give between Me and between you, and between all living souls that are with you, for all generations. I put My rainbow in the cloud, and it will be a sign of the covenant between Me and the earth."[1]*

The rainbow is shaped like a hunting bow that faces away from earth. This reminds us that the world sometimes deserves to be destroyed by a flood, but God's compassion reduces the flow of water to a mere rainstorm.

Implications for Us

When disasters come to the world, we should take stock of how we might improve our behavior. Nothing happens by accident, and "natural disasters" such as floods, earthquakes, tsunamis, and volcanic eruptions are supposed to send us messages.

A rainbow results from a bright, white light splitting into its component colors. We all come from the same divine Source, yet have our individual roles and contributions to make to the world. When people stop appreciating and respecting the divine image in others and ourselves and neglect the divine plan for living, the Almighty will respond to us. We should always wonder if disasters are meant to be a wake-up call for us to live differently.

When we hear about natural disasters, the best responses we can have are to make sure that we are living the way that we should. Meanwhile, we should do our utmost to relieve others' suffering. When we show compassion to others, we can ask the Almighty to do the same to us.

Notes
1.   Genesis 9:11-13.

Indulgence

After God assured Noah that He would never again destroy the world by water, Noah planted a grapevine so that he could sanctify wine by using it to serve the Almighty. His Creator warned Noah that Adam had misused grapes in the Garden of Eden,[1] yet Noah paid no heed.

> *And Noah, man of the ground, began and planted a vineyard. And he drank from the wine and he became drunk, and he was uncovered in the midst of his tent. And Ham, the father of Canaan saw the nakedness of his father, and he told his two brothers outside. And Shem and Yaffet took the blanket, and they put it on the shoulders of the two of them, and they went backwards, and they covered their father's nakedness, and their faces were backwards, and they didn't see their father's nakedness.*
>
> *And Noah woke up from his wine, and he knew what his youngest son had done to him. And he said, "Cursed be Canaan, a slave of slaves will he be to his brothers." And he said, "Blessed is the Lord, the God of Shem. And may Canaan be a servant to him. May God enlarge Yaffet, and he should dwell in the tents of Shem, and let Canaan be a servant to him."[2]*

Once again, God advised man, man didn't listen to Him, and man suffered terrible consequences. The Master of the World sees the long-term consequences of everything we do; we are often blind to them.

The Torah describes this episode using two terms that have sexual connotations: "he was uncovered" and he "knew." These imply that Noah cursed Ham and Canaan because they committed some type of sexual crime with Noah, their father and grandfather, respectively.

The Midrash[3] and Rashi say that Ham didn't want his father to sire any more children. It was bad enough that Ham would have to share the world with two other siblings—he certainly didn't want there to be any others with whom to share it! Now that the family had left the ark, Noah wanted to repopulate the world. Before he went to be with his wife, Noah drank too much wine. Ham exploited his father's drunken stupor by castrating Noah so that Ham's share wouldn't be diminished by Noah having more offspring.

Canaan, on the other hand, sodomized Noah, his grandfather, when Noah was under the influence of alcohol. When Noah came back to his senses, he cursed Canaan for his indecent behavior.[4]

Implications for Us

The Torah has many laws that make sense. Most civilized people today would say that it is wrong to steal, murder, or oppress the helpless, widows, and orphans. Yet, people often define whom it is wrong to steal from or murder in self-serving ways. A few decades ago, much of the civilized world believed that it was fine to experiment on or murder mentally retarded people and Jews. A century ago, blacks in many parts of the Western world were also regarded as "non-humans." It was the Torah that gave the Western world definitions of morality that truly respect the dignity of human beings, especially those that are powerless, in ways that are still unmatched by any other culture.

The Torah and Jewish tradition also caution about the potential harmful effects of alcohol. While alcohol can elevate man's spirit, its misuse can lead to disaster.

It is ironic that despite the Torah's track record in civilizing the world and teaching people the importance of self-control, few Jews appreciate that a Torah way of life and thinking has done so much to better the world. They read laws in the Torah that don't make sense or that they don't like and assume that they can devise a better system using their own logic. Many enlightened people insist that the Torah's laws were only relevant to ancient, primitive people, and they use their God-given intelligence and free will to reject what He commanded us to do!

The Torah expresses God's wisdom, the greatest logic that there is. We must be humble to accept that He knows better than we do how to make the most of our lives. Throughout history, people have assumed that divine laws didn't apply to them, and then discovered that they were mistaken. For example, the Torah prohibited Jewish kings from having too many wives or too many horses, lest the wives turn the king away from God or the king send Jews back to Egypt to get horses. King Solomon reasoned that since he was the wisest of all men, these laws didn't apply to him. He ended up marrying too many women (1,000 wives and concubines altogether) and amassed too many horses by sending Jews to Egypt to get them. His descendants lost their reign over the entire Jewish nation because he allowed his wives to practice idolatry, which later spread throughout the Jewish kingdom and led to the Jews' ruin and exile.

If we want to avoid making mistakes, we can learn from Adam's and Noah's errors and live by the rules and wise counsel that God gave us for our benefit. Our judgment can never be better than His.

Noah made a terrible mistake. He miscalculated how alcohol would affect him when he drank to escape his devastation and feelings of being overwhelmed by a world in which everything was destroyed. He let his emotions override God's advice to him, with disastrous consequences. His son and grandson learned nothing from the Flood about the critical importance of rising above their jealousy, passion, and animalistic instincts, and they exploited his powerlessness.

The Almighty holds us responsible when we put ourselves in harm's way because we want thrills, money, comfort, or pleasure, or when we use destructive means to respond to life's challenges. God wants us to use our free will and intelligence to make wise choices that help us master our emotions, cope with our pain, and rebuild our lives after tragedy strikes.

Many people use alcohol and drugs to avoid unpleasant feelings. There is a strong idea in the Western world today that life is about having pleasure or living comfortably, instead of accepting that life is supposed to have challenges and sometimes be uncomfortable. God wants us to successfully confront challenges by becoming people who grow spiritually (if not in other ways) as we cope with painful, difficult, or disappointing situations.

God sends us challenges and difficulties throughout our lives. Most of our important accomplishments result from overcoming them. Alcohol, drugs, and other short-term panaceas never help us develop our spiritual potentials. To the contrary, if we confuse our minds to a point where we can't make proper moral choices, Noah's example tells us that negative consequences are likely to follow.

When we feel overwhelmed by life as Noah did, we should talk to our Creator. Just as food nourishes the body, prayer nourishes the soul's connection with its Source. We can turn to God in our pain and ask for direction, support, and closeness with Him. Our Heavenly Parent, like any loving caretaker, wants nothing more than to give His children what they need most. What we need, though, is not necessarily what we want. When we open ourselves to hearing the divine will for us and how we should respond to our challenges, we are already on the path to finding a solution.

Notes
1. *Genesis Rabbah* 36.
2. Genesis 9:20-27.
3. *Genesis Rabbah* 36.
4. *Oznaim L'torah* on Genesis 9:18. Canaan's descendants were well known for their sexual immorality.

The Tower of Babel

Years after the Flood, the world became repopulated, and we might think that people tried their best to live up to the original divine plan for humanity. Unfortunately, that is not what happened. Instead of appreciating the importance of following the Seven Noahide Principles of morality (ethical monotheism), people began a new project to thwart God's will:

> *All the earth was of one tongue* [safah] *and of one set of words* [devarim achadim]. *And it was when they traveled from kedem and found a valley in the land of Shinar, they settled there. And the people said to one another, "Let us build bricks, and we will burn it into an inferno, and the brick will be for a building block . . ." Then they said, "Let us build a city and a tower with its peak in heaven, and we will make a name for ourselves, lest we spread out upon the face of the earth."*[1]

This story seems rather strange. If we notice the exact wording, we will see that Genesis says that the earth was "of one tongue" instead of saying that everyone spoke the same language. Since God wrote the Torah, and none of its details are irrelevant, what does He want us to know by saying this? Also, why did He say that people traveled from *kedem* to build a tower, and that it reached the heavens?

We should also wonder why these people built a tower in a valley. And why did they burn bricks into an inferno, instead of making an inferno so that they could manufacture bricks?

We can start answering these questions by analyzing what *kedem* means. *Kedem* usually means "east," but there is no reason for Genesis to tell us where these people came from. *Kedem* here must have a different meaning.

Kedem can sometimes mean "before," or "preceding," so the Midrash says that *kedem* alludes to the people of Babel moving away from the *kadmono shel olam*—the One who preceded the world. In other words, people built the Tower of Babel to rebel against God.[2]

This idea is bolstered by using the phrase "one tongue" to indicate that everyone spoke the same language.[3] Had the Torah only wanted us to know that the world was unilingual, it would have used the customary Hebrew word for language—*lashon*. Instead, it uses the word *safah* to teach us something else.

Safah refers to words that emanate from the lips or mouth, while *lashon* are words that come from the tongue. *Safah* are words that are external to a person—i.e., superficial speech. *Lashon* are words that come from deep within and express our essence.

Saying that the people of Babel all spoke one *safah* means that they spoke superficially, without relating to language's deeper, spiritual purpose. In other words, they spoke to further their self-interests. They didn't use Hebrew as the holy tongue (*lashon hakodesh*) that it was intended to be. Genesis uses the word *safah* to express that they were hypocrites who only gave "lip service" to their words.

The spiritual purpose of speech is to reveal God's Presence in the world and to connect us to Him and to one another in positive ways. Their purpose in speaking was to connect to each other so that they could escape or overthrow God's dominion.

Implications for Us

We usually take the divine gift of speech for granted. In some ways, Judaism equates being able to speak with being alive. Genesis says that when God made Adam, "the man became a living being."[4] The commentator Onkelos[5] explained that Adam becoming a "living being" meant that he became a "speaking being."

The Torah has 31 commandments that tell us how to speak to, or about, others. We must be careful not to speak in ways that harm ourselves or others.[6] This means not gossiping, and considering before we speak if our words will be hurtful or trivialize others. If they will, it is best not to say anything at all. As King Solomon said, "Closing one's lips makes a person wise."[7] Rabbi Shimon ben Gamliel said, "All my days I grew up among the wise men, and I have found nothing greater (for the body) than silence."[8] Or as Mark Twain wryly penned, "It is better to keep your mouth closed and let people think you are a fool than to open it and remove all doubt."

Words are supposed to bring the divine Presence into the world and make the world a more harmonious and holy place. If we have not spoken that way until now, it is never too late to start.

Notes

1. Genesis 11:1-4.
2. *Genesis Rabbah* 38.
3. Rashi on Genesis 11:1 says that the original language spoken by Adam and his descendants was Hebrew.
4. Genesis 2:7.
5. He was the nephew of a Roman emperor and a convert to Judaism.
6. There are specific occasions when one may speak truthfully about someone who is evil (as defined by Jewish law) or may give negative factual information about a potential marriage or business partner to protect people from harm. The details of such instances are delineated in the Chofetz Chaim's book, *Guard Your Tongue*, translated by Rabbi Zelig Pliskin, New York, Moriah Offset, 1977.
7. Proverbs 10:19.
8. *Ethics of the Fathers* 1:17.

Idolatry vs. Monotheism

The Torah frequently mentions that most of the world's people were idolaters, something that few Westerners can conceive of today. The reason that we can't conceive of it is because of the changes that an ancient man named Abraham brought to the world. His ideas still affect the world today.

To appreciate who Abraham was, and the world into which he was born, we need to know about his contemporaries and about the society they created.

People often think that ancient Biblical people were idolaters or were immoral because they were primitive, yet that isn't the case. Ancient Near Eastern people were sophisticated in many areas of life. People's level of morality has had little to do with their agricultural, business, or scientific sophistication. Some of the most powerful, wealthy, and technologically advanced countries have been the most immoral as well. We only have to look at 20th-century Nazi Germany to see that. People have not changed as much as we might think over thousands of years.

The Akkadians, later known as the people of Babel, were one of the first civilizations. They imported bitumen, copper, silver, gold, calcite, limestone, and alabaster. They even brought in lapus lazuli, a beautiful blue stone used in jewelry and decorating, from 1,500 miles away! Their metropolis of Ur had a population close to 35,000 people, with a surrounding population of another 250,000-500,000. The town contained over 4,000 houses.

The empire of Ur was a trading and manufacturing center with some 40 districts, an elaborate bureaucratic structure, a court, a legal system, and sophisticated accounting and guild systems. Far from being a backward group of tent-dwellers, the people were bankers and traders. Their records give us some idea of how developed their industries were: Nearly 9,000 slaves worked in Ur's textile industry. One weaving factory made 12 different kinds of woolen cloth. One king alone imported and stored over a quarter million bushels of grain. One bookkeeping center recorded trading 350,000 sheep and over 28,000 cattle in one year.[1]

This was the world into which Abraham was born almost four thousand years ago. He grew up in Ur Kasdim and lived during the time of the Tower of Babel, nearly 2,000 years after Adam was created. By then, almost everyone in the world was idolatrous because they believed that worshipping statues and the like would ensure that nature would give its bounty. To them, the proof was in the pudding. Look how successful they were!

Yet Abraham, whose father was an idol salesman, came to believe in one God. How? He looked at the complexity of the world and at various forces of nature (the sun, moon, stars, and so on), and realized that none of them was all-powerful. He reasoned that there must be a single Creator who was totally powerful, who continually supervised and guided the world, and who created everything because He wanted a relationship with people. Abraham figured out that the only way for mankind to truly relate to God was to know what He wanted from us and to do it.

Abraham lived on the northern part of a major trade route in the Fertile Crescent. Armed with his intellectual understanding of who God was, Abraham's geographical placement gave him an unparalleled opportunity to teach large numbers of idolaters about ethical monotheism. Thus, it was not coincidental that Abraham lived where he did.

When Abraham was in his seventies, the Almighty asked him to move to the land of Canaan, which God had situated between the ancient world's superpowers, in the center of a world trade route. Abraham moved to the Holy Land, which bridged Asia and Africa. That was an ideal location from which divine teachings could be spread around the world.

The prosperous, sophisticated, and metropolitan inhabitants of Ur were the people of Babel who built a tower to displace the One Above and make themselves into gods. They waged a spiritual, more than physical, battle against the Almighty.

Genesis alludes to this by saying that the entire world was of one language and of *devarim achadim* prior to their building this tower.

While *devarim achadim* can mean "of one speech," it literally means "single words."

Devarim achadim can also mean "singular individuals." The people of Babel wanted to wage war against special individuals. The Midrash[2] says that these singular individuals were the One Above and Abraham. Just as God was unique in Heaven, Abraham was unique in bringing Heaven down to earth. He was a monotheist who tried to convince a pagan world to abandon their idolatrous and immoral beliefs and believe in ethical monotheism instead.

The purpose of the Tower of Babel, then, was to rebel against God and Abraham's teachings about Him. A Jewish legend fleshes out this story:

When Abraham was a child, he wanted to show his father, who sold idols, that believing in idols was ridiculous. One day, his father went away for a few hours. Meanwhile, Abraham took a hammer and destroyed all but the biggest idol in his father's store. Abraham then left the hammer in the hand of that idol. When his father came back and found that all of his merchandise had been smashed, he fumed at Abraham, "Who did this?"

Abraham replied, "The idols got into an argument and the biggest one smashed all of the other ones."

His father replied, "That's ridiculous. Everyone knows that an idol can't do anything."

Abraham responded, "Let your ears hear what your mouth speaks. If an idol is so powerless that it can't even destroy another idol, why worship it?"

As punishment for his iconoclasm, Abraham was brought to King Nimrod, the ruler of Babel. *Nimrod*, whose name means "let us rebel," was totally opposed to Abraham's ideology. After all, part of his pagan people's belief system was that their king was a god. If they stopped believing in pagan superstition and magic, they would also regard their king as a mere mortal. Clearly, Abraham was a threat to Nimrod's aspirations.[3]

Nimrod's desire for honor ruined the world. He endangered others with his scheme to make himself, rather than the All-Powerful One, a deity to his people. It was he who encouraged people to make a brick oven whose real purpose was to immolate Abraham before Abraham's philosophy could topple Nimrod. When the brick furnace was finished, Nimrod made an inferno inside and threw Abraham in. God miraculously saved Abraham for trusting Him.[4]

This is one explanation as to why the Torah says that the people of Babel made bricks to have a fire, rather than making fire to fashion bricks. This also explains why they built a tower in a valley that "reached Heaven." The people were not interested in building a city. They only wanted to destroy belief in God.

Why did these people want to rebel against God? They decided that He was undependable.[5] After all, He destroyed the world with a flood once. Why shouldn't He bring another calamity to destroy most of the world again?

The people of Babel didn't want to accept responsibility for the consequences of their misbehavior. If there would be another calamity, it must be God's fault. When they got a message that they didn't like from Abraham—i.e., that there was a Creator who expected them to act morally—they tried to shoot the messenger. Instead of improving themselves as a guaranteed way to prevent future calamities, they tried to remove the All-Powerful One's dominion over them.

Adam had been told, "Be fruitful, and multiply, and fill the earth and conquer it [nature]."[6] The One Above deliberately made people vulnerable to nature's tornadoes, floods, drought, disease, and the like so that these disasters would get us to soul-search and grow.

When God told Adam to conquer nature, He didn't mean that Adam should destroy the environment. He meant that people should live according to the Creator's will so that nature will always provide what we need. The Almighty designed nature in a way that it would automatically take care of us if we live according to the divine plan. In the ideal world, nature only harms us when we let our physical desires dominate our spirituality. Our misbehavior fritters away the ability to overcome nature that connecting to God gives us.

Like their predecessors, the people of Babel did not want to improve themselves morally. They wanted to solve all of their problems by making themselves gods who would not have to rely on a Higher Power.

Unfortunately for them, God ultimately reigns supreme. Their scheme only resulted in their losing the power that could have been theirs had they only connected themselves to the Source.

Implications for Us

Nimrod was no different from many modern leaders and scientists. He wanted to control the world and remove people's need to believe in God. While such people often succeed to a point, their attempts to eradicate belief in a Supreme Deity eventually break down. Sooner or later, people search for greater meaning in life as they see that human power invariably ends up being corrupt and that human beings are no match for nature.

If we would only seek greater meaning and think about the One Above before disasters befall us, many of those disasters would not need to come at all.

Notes

1. The information about the Akkadians and Ur appears in Samuel Kurinsky, *The Eighth Day*, Northvale, NJ, Jason Aronson, 1994, pp. 37-39.
2. *Genesis Rabbah* 38:6.
3. *Otzar Hetefillot*, "Introduction to the *Amidah*," refers to this story.
4. *Genesis Rabbah* 38:13 recounts this episode. Abraham was 52 years old at the time the tower of Babel was built.
5. Rashi on Genesis 11:1, quoting *Genesis Rabbah* 38.
6. Genesis 1:28.

United We Stand

Nimrod was an evil king, yet his desire to unite the world's people (albeit in rebelling against God) was positive. He was sure that a united people would have so much collective strength that they wouldn't need to rely on a supreme deity. We shall see that he was right about the strength that people have when they are united:

> *Then the Lord came down to see the city and the tower that the people built. And the Lord said, "Behold, it is one nation with one language, and this is the beginning of what they will do. And now, nothing will be withheld from them of what they will scheme to do. Let us go down and mix up their language so that a man will not understand his neighbor's language." And the Lord spread them from there across the face of the earth and they stopped building the city.*[1]

We learn from this episode that people's unity wields tremendous power, even if they come together for bad reasons. The power of unity is implied by the fact that the One Above intervened in the Babelites' plan—otherwise, it would have worked! Even today, we see the incredible strength that people have if they only work together for a common cause instead of being fragmented by their differences.

Since the people of Babel misused their unity and common language by trying to destroy morality, God punished them "measure for measure." He took away their unity by making them speak different languages and spreading them across the earth. He then infused them with nationalistic feelings that didn't exist before.

Although people can use nationalistic feelings positively, these have historically motivated wars and killing those with different beliefs, skin color, and lineage. Nationalism has spurred people to risk life and limb for their countries, even when there were no ideals at stake that were worth defending.[2]

Before such nationalism existed, people only fought locally. With the advent of nationalism, people began destroying each other across the face of the earth. Misdirected nationalistic feelings have been humanity's scourge ever since.

The world's people generally, and the Jews specifically, could accomplish almost anything if we would only see our commonalities and work together for common goals. If we would do this, we could eradicate a great deal of suffering through medical and technological developments and education that are shared worldwide. We have tremendous strength in numbers. God had to thwart the Babelites' plan because their success as a unified people in building the world's first skyscraper would have led them to believe themselves to be invincible and in no need of a Heavenly Ruler. Next, they would have become totally corrupt and once again derailed the world from its spiritual mission.

Implications for Us

Prosperity, technological sophistication, and knowledge never guarantee morality. Maimonides said that when people are so prosperous that they have lots of leisure time, they are likely to do spiritually destructive things to fill the void.[3]

Instead of appreciating the One who made them prosper, the people of Babel did the opposite. They mistrusted and resented Him. It is part of human nature to want more and more. Unfortunately, once we get what we want, we often resent the very people who helped us achieve our desires.

The story of the tower of Babel underscores humanity's fear of relying on and being accountable to God. Our nature is to fight our Creator's authority and proclaim self-rule. When we don't want to rely on Him, we should know that the alternatives are always much worse.

One lesson of the Tower of Babel is that when people deify themselves and try to displace God, they eventually try to dominate and destroy others. The second lesson is that when people agree on a goal and pursue it, their unity can create enormous strength. If we join together to make the world a more moral and spiritually wholesome place, our combined efforts will reap amazing results.

Notes
1. Genesis 11:5-8.
2. For example, Assyria battled Babylonia, various Greek city-states fought one another, the Greeks fought the Persians, then the Romans, and so on. One did not spread greater morality or decency than the others.
3. Personal communication to the author by Rabbi Yitzchok Kirzner, z"tl, in 1990 at the Jewish Renaissance Center.

Appendix

Who Wrote the Five Books of Moses?

Jews and Christians originally believed that God authored the Torah and that it was neither man-made nor merely divinely inspired. During the Enlightenment, some Christians began to question this. In the 1800s, an anti-Semitic German Protestant theologian named Wellhausen created the "documentary hypothesis." He insisted that the Five Books of Moses consisted of different writing styles, which he attributed to multiple authors who lived between 950 and 400 BCE. He claimed that "J" wrote the narratives, as well as the sections referring to God as *Ado-nai*; "E" wrote sections that referred to God as *Elo-him*; "P" wrote laws relating to priests and the Tabernacle; and "D" wrote Deuteronomy. Then, "R" (for "redactor") supposedly wove these fragments together into one book. Bible critics used this theory to explain–

1. Why parts of the Torah seem redundant or have inconsistencies, such as the two Creation stories in Genesis.
2. Why the Torah refers to God using different names, especially Ado-nai and Elo-him.
3. Why parts of the Torah seem to have different styles and foci, such that Genesis contains mostly narratives, while Leviticus lists many ritual laws, especially those applicable to priests and the Tabernacle.
4. Why the Torah discusses events and people that existed after Moses' death, such as eight Edomite kings who lived after Moses died, or that Moses died and no one knows where he was buried.
5. Why the Torah has anachronisms. For example, Bible critics insist that Abraham could not have owned camels because camels were not domesticated until centuries after he lived.

In light of these discrepancies, is it rational to believe that the Torah was given by God and penned by Moses? The answer is a resounding yes. Parts of this book series will address some of these theories. For now, we will objectively respond to a few of these criticisms.

To test the idea that the Five Books of Moses were multiply authored, a researcher did a computer analysis of the Torah and other books. Comparing Torah sections that critics claim were written by separate authors, the computer looked at 54 variables and concluded that there was an 82% probability that one author had written them. By contrast, there was only an 8% probability that Kant had written Kant, and a 22% probability that Goethe had written Goethe![1]

Neither Biblical nor modern books need be written in only one style, and our modern conception of what a book should look like is different from that of a book that has been relevant to people for more than 3,000 years.

Traditional medieval (Rashi, Nachmanides, Sforno, and Ibn Ezra) and modern Jewish commentators (such as Cassuto) also raised, and addressed, many of the difficulties that led the Bible critics to the documentary hypothesis. The interested reader should see these commentaries on the verses in question, as they are beyond the scope of this book.

Discrepancies and Redundancies

Judaism teaches that a perfect God revealed His "thoughts" through a Torah that has no mistakes, superfluities, or redundant letters or words. While modern Bible critics maintain that the Bible has many mistakes due to human editing errors and anachronisms, ancient traditional Jewish commentaries taught that these seeming "errors" were deliberately planted by God to encourage us to mine the riches of His insights into us and the world.

The Torah's supposed inconsistencies prompt us to search ever deeper into God's revealed "thoughts." Many interpretations can be correct, just as a diamond's many facets can appear different yet all be part of the same beautiful gem.

Anachronisms and Dating

When Bible critics, historians, or archaeologists say that certain events in the Torah never happened, or occurred later than the Torah said they happened, their conclusions are usually based on what historians and archaeologists *didn't* discovered. However, lack of evidence is not evidence of a lack. If we don't find something, it doesn't prove that it never existed or never happened; it only means that we haven't found it yet. There are countless instances of archaeological finds changing archaeologists' theories overnight. For example, historians before the latter half of the twentieth century didn't know that entire civilizations existed, such as Ebla. When archaeologists haven't found artifacts such as bones, pottery, homes, or written records corroborating Biblical events, they have often jumped to hasty and wrong conclusions, insisting that the Bible's authors made up those stories. A few reasons why archaeologists and historians come to incorrect conclusions:

1. There are no objective criteria for determining that someone is qualified to give expert opinions about the authenticity, or lack thereof, of the Bible. For example, an entire group (the Copenhagen School) of "Bible scholars" are neither archaeologists nor can they even read Hebrew! How can someone be an expert about a text that he or she can't even read?

2. Today, especially in places like Tel Aviv University, many Bible critics and archaeologists have formulated the most absurd of theories, whose main intent seems to be to invalidate belief in the Jewish Bible's divinity. Their ideas are popular in many academic and left-wing arenas and have filtered down to lay people and books. Popularity with the masses does not prove the theories' validity. Unfortunately, the secularists' hatred toward religious Jews and religious observance makes it politically incorrect to fund work or publicize findings that support the authenticity of Jewish Scriptures. For example, Adam Zertal, a secular archaeologist, discovered an altar on Mt. Eval. Its dimensions, artifacts

(especially burnt bones from kosher animals), and dating conformed exactly to the altar that Joshua built there. When Zertal concluded that he had found Joshua's altar, he was ridiculed by other secular archaeologists.

3. Eilat Mazar recently excavated what she claims was the palace of King David, at the top of the city of David. She found an enormous building, fit for a king, with pottery from the correct era and Phoenician stone masonry that is consistent with the Biblical account. As he typically does whenever archeological finds substantiate the Jewish Bible, Israel Finkelstein of Tel Aviv University declared soon after her announcement that it couldn't possibly date to David's time, and must be from a different era.

4. The annals of Biblical historians and archaeologists are filled with ongoing arguments about almost every aspect of Biblical criticism and validation, the meaning and significance of artifacts that have been found, the dating of finds and events, and so on. There is almost never a consensus between them. What is certain today is often rejected within a decade.

5. Maximalist archaeologists believe that research has largely supported the Torah's authenticity, especially its narratives. Minimalists do not believe this. William Albright, a maximalist, once concluded, "Numerous recent excavations in sites in this period in Palestine, supplemented by finds made in Egypt and Syria, give us a remarkably precise idea of patriarchal Palestine, fitting well into the picture handed down in Genesis."[2]

6. It often happens that a site is excavated and conclusions are made about the findings that discredit our Bible. After excavating elsewhere, archaeologists are sometimes forced to conclude that the Biblical (time of the Prophets) description was correct after maintaining for years that it was wrong. For example, Kathleen Kenyon, a noted minimalist archaeologist, concluded that Jericho was never the major city the Book of Joshua says it was. It turned out that she had conducted her dig in the wrong place, leaving half of the ancient city buried

and unscrutinized![3] She made a number of other seriously wrong conclusions about other archaeological sites as well. One of these was to insist that the ancient city of Jerusalem was a small village. She dismissed as fanciful myths the Biblical stories that said the city expanded to the "Machtesh" and the "Mishnah" (areas to the north and west of Jerusalem) after the exile of the northern Jews by the Assyrians. Later archaeological digs in Jerusalem showed that the city was indeed large enough to support 30,000-40,000 inhabitants, if not twice that amount, and that it had expanded to the northwest and west as the Bible described.

7. Archaeologists have initially misidentified, misunderstood, or misdated many an ancient site, city, grave, tower, and so on. For example, the famous Dead Sea Scrolls were originally thought to have been medieval. It was only when similar scrolls were found at Masada that they were properly dated at about 1,000 years earlier.

    It used to be taught that the Romans invented the arch. Excavations in Israel revealed two massive arches dating back to the 18th century BCE, more than 1,000 years earlier than the Romans.

    It was once taught that David's general, Yoav, entered Jerusalem and conquered it from the Jebusites by entering through a tunnel known as Warren's Shaft. Less than a decade ago, a more thorough excavation revealed that he couldn't have entered that way because it was covered by a layer of rock in his time, which was chiseled away more than 200 years later.

    The Waqf illegally excavated 200 tons of material from the Temple Mount a few years ago. They removed artifacts and dumped the rest into the Kidron Valley, where they mixed much of it with garbage. We don't know what critical finds the Waqf removed, and they made it impossible to definitively date finds that they didn't remove. Nevertheless, some of the finds that were recovered will necessitate historians rewriting books that discuss how the Temple Mount was used during the Byzantine era.

We should not think that archaeology is an exact science, or expect archaeologists or historians to know everything there is to know about a site or a civilization. Lay people should know that the conclusions archeologists draw are typically theories, not facts, and there is a context in which they base their conclusions. For example,

1. Only 23% of original artifacts survive over time. The rest erode or disintegrate.
2. Nomadic societies, such as the ancient Israelites or traditional Bedouins, do not leave artifacts behind.
3. Secular and Christian Biblical archaeologists and historians don't study traditional Jewish commentaries on the Bible, the Talmud, or the myriad of ancient books such as *Seder Olam*, which is the only continual history book of the world. Nor do they typically consult with those rabbinic scholars who have a wealth of information about what traditional Jewish sources have to say about the history of the land of Israel and its sites, Jewish history, or artifacts and how they were used. One would think that the secular archaeologists who use our Bible to locate sites and what occurred there would also use the same written Bible plus our traditions to interpret and understand our history and their finds, but they don't. Instead of assuming that our people were the best historians and our Bible and traditions are informed, they give credence to other civilizations or their own logic instead. When other civilizations have nothing to say about us, the secularists still dismiss our traditions as having no validity.
4. The way that archaeologists sample an area when they dig means it is not necessarily representative of an entire settlement. Only a tiny part of ancient Israel (and the ancient Fertile Crescent) has ever been excavated. When ancient settlements are found and excavated, only about 1% of the artifacts of a settlement are ever uncovered. Conclusions

about that settlement and civilization are made based on the 1% of artifacts that are found! If someone found 1% of our house and only 1/4% of our belongings, would his or her conclusions about us and our lives be accurate?

5. Archaeologists have found artifacts only the last day of some digs (such as Ekron), giving them critical information that totally changed their understanding of the site. In general, we don't know how much information remains undiscovered that would change other facts that are "known."

6. Ancient people did not leave many written records because few people were literate, and there were a limited number of scribes who knew how to write. Many civilizations passed down their oral traditions from generation to generation and did not record them. Thousands of years ago, there were no copying machines, printing presses, daily newspapers, or magazines, so the amount of written material was minuscule compared to today. When written records were kept on parchment or forms of paper, the organic materials on which they were written usually disintegrated over time. Except for unusual circumstances where documents were preserved in dry and unmolested storage rooms, the only ancient writing to survive appeared on pottery or stone, or as paintings and writings on tombs or in caves. Little of this from 3,000 years ago in Israel has been found. Not finding written traces from a group of people is not proof that they didn't exist, only that we have not found their records. The fact that the Torah we have today is virtually identical to those parchments that survived from 2,000 years ago in the Dead Sea Scrolls is good substantiation to our claims that the Torah we have today is the same one that we were given at Mount Sinai.

With that as background, let's now be scientific and scrutinize some of the Bible critics' theories. When early Bible critics made up their documentary hypothesis, they maintained that the Torah could not have been written when Jewish tradition says it was, in 1312 BCE. The critics used the fact that the earliest scrolls found with phonetic script were dated to 1000 BCE to conclude that the Torah could not have been written earlier than that. The basis for their claims collapsed, however, when the Tel el Amarna Letters and other manuscripts were found that dated back to the time that the Torah was given, and earlier. These documents proved that people in the Torah's era wrote in phonetic script, so it was not anachronistic for the Torah to have been written when it claimed it was. However, the critics did not revise their dating of our books as a result of this discovery.

The minimalist school also insists that parts of the Five Books of Moses were authored as recently as the fifth century BCE. When archaeologist Gabi Barkay excavated the tombs of Kettef Hinnom (behind today's Begin Center in Jerusalem), he discovered two amulets with the Biblical priestly blessing from the Book of Numbers written on them, dating to the 7th century BCE. The Torah's verses were obviously written much earlier, insofar as they were so well known by the 7th century BCE that people were wearing them for protection. Not only that, but a sophisticated laboratory at a California university analyzed the silver and showed that it also contained verses from the Book of Deuteronomy. The critics had maintained that the Book of Deuteronomy was written much later and didn't exist at that time. Thus, one archaeological find buried the minimalists' misdating of the Torah as well as their ideas about Deuteronomy, yet people continue to teach the outdated ideas as if they were true.

Archaeologists generally believe that statements in Genesis describing Abraham as having domesticated camels are anachronistic. When Albright made this claim, he based it on the fact that the earliest *texts* found that discuss domesticated camels dated from the 11th century BCE. Abraham lived around eight to nine hundred years earlier. Today, all academics "know" that Abraham's camels in the Book of Genesis are an anachronism.

Yet there is proof that Bactrian (Asian) camels were domesticated between 2500 and 1900 BCE, and dromedaries (Arabian camels) were domesticated not later than 2150 BCE. We know the latter from a rock painting found near Aswan in 1912 that shows a man leading a dromedary with a rope, with hieroglyphic characters that date it to 2200 BCE or earlier.[4] This predates Abraham's lifetime by about 500 years. It is likely that camels were a luxury item for hundreds of years that were only owned by wealthy people. That may be why non-Biblical texts found so far only mention them later.

Archaeological Surveys in Samaria

From the 1970s until the 1990s, teams of secular archaeologists and students combed the West Bank and examined pottery shards that had worked their way to the surface. They found enough information to see a comprehensive picture of ancient settlements in the Biblical heartland for the first time, including these details:[5]

1. Towns described in the Jewish Bible were exactly where they were supposed to be. This information could not have been known to documentary hypothesis authors because many of these cities were long buried, and later generations would not have known about them.
2. The Jewish Bible's descriptions of local customs are accurate for the periods that are described. For example, historical documents have been found which show that Joseph was sold as a slave for the amount of money that a man his age fetched on the slave market. By the time the hypothetical Biblical authors lived, prices were very different, and the earlier customs were already forgotten.
3. The Jewish Bible is so accurate in its historical descriptions that it is used to locate archaeological sites throughout the land of Israel.

Predictions

If God wrote the Torah, the fact that it predicted events that would happen after Moses' death is not problematic. God knows everything that has and that will happen, from the Creation of the world until its end.

Bible critics are troubled by the Torah mentioning Edomite kings who would reign in the future because they don't believe that the Torah was given by the Almighty. Yet they ignore that the Torah accurately foretold, in great detail, what would happen to the Jewish people for millennia to come. No human being could, or would dare, make these predictions because they defy normal expectations. Here are but two examples:

The Torah predicted the Babylonian and Roman exiles that the Jews would endure if they didn't obey the Torah. The documentary hypothesis says that the Torah appeared about five hundred years before the Roman conquest of the Holy Land and exile of the Jews. At the time the Bible critics say the Five Books of Moses were put together, most Jews lived far from Israel, under Babylonian or Persian rule. Only 40,000 Jews returned to Israel from the Diaspora when Cyrus allowed it. The overwhelming majority stayed outside the Land. How could a human redactor of the Torah living in Asia have predicted the specific, unique, and unthinkable events that would happen under Roman rule hundreds of years later? We don't find the author of the United States Constitution making accurate predictions about what would happen in America hundreds of years later. But that is exactly what Deuteronomy foretells in this section following the description of the bounty and blessing that the Jews would enjoy if they followed the Torah:[6]

> *If you don't listen to the voice of the Lord your God, and are not careful to guard and observe all of the commandments and ritual laws that I command you today . . . the Lord will send you curse . . . and trouble in everything you do because you abandoned Me. The Lord will allow you to be beaten down in front of your enemies . . . and you will be a terrifying example to all the kingdoms of the earth. . . . You will build a house and not live in it. You will plant a vineyard and not harvest the grapes. Your ox will be slaughtered in front of your eyes, and you will not eat of it. . . . Your flocks will be given to your enemies, and you will have none to save them. Your sons and daughters will be given to another nation. Your eyes will see it and long for them all day long, but you will have no strength. The fruit of*

your ground and all of your labors will be devoured by a nation you don't know. . . .

The Lord will bring you, and the king you have set over yourselves, to a nation that neither you nor your ancestors have known. You will serve other gods there, of wood and rock. You will be an astonishment . . . and a topic of conversation to all of the nations where the Lord your God will lead you. . . . You shall give birth to sons and daughters, but they will not be yours, because they will go into captivity. . . .

All of this will happen . . . because you did not listen to the Lord your God's voice, to observe His commandments and His ordinances. These events will be a sign . . . upon your seed forever that you did not serve the Lord your God with happiness and a joyful heart when you had great abundance. Instead, famished, thirsty, naked, and lacking everything, you will serve enemies whom the Lord will send against you. . . .

The Lord will bring a nation from afar . . . as the eagle soars, a nation whose language you will not understand. A brazen nation who will show no deference to the elderly, and will have no compassion for the young.

They will eat your animals and produce until you are annihilated. They will leave you no corn, wine, oil, cattle, or flocks, and they will destroy you.

They will besiege you in all of your gates until your high and fortified walls, where you placed your trust, come down throughout your land. . . . You will eat your children . . . because of the siege and straits that you are in. . . .

And you shall remain few in number, whereas you had been as numerous as the stars of the heavens, because you did not listen to the Lord your God. . . . He will scatter you among all of the nations, from one end of the earth to the other.

You will have no peace of mind among the nations . . . because of . . . what you will witness.

The Lord will send you back to Egypt in ships by the path that I said you would never see again. You will be sold there as male and female slaves for your enemies but no one will buy you.

These predictions all came true in the first century CE and subsequently.[7] How so? The Romans were the nation that came from afar, whose Latin language the Jews didn't know, and whose symbol was the eagle.

The Romans were ruthless and didn't respect the young or old. As Josephus wrote, "No pity was shown to age or rank, old men or children, the laity or priests—all were massacred. . . . The ground was hidden by corpses, and the soldiers had to climb over heaps of bodies . . . ."[8]

The Romans destroyed all of the vineyards and fruit-bearing trees they found in Israel in order to remove the Jews' food source. ["You will plant a vineyard and not harvest the grapes."] The Romans plowed salt into the soil so that nothing would grow there again. The formerly lush land of Israel was so desolate after the Roman attack, it barely grew anything until the Jews repopulated Israel in large numbers more than 1800 years later.

The Romans besieged Jerusalem in 66 CE. During their three-year siege, Jews and their livestock died of starvation and disease. As Josephus wrote, ". . . countless thousands of Jews died of hunger. In every house where there was the least morsel of food, relatives fought over it. . . . Then there was the incredible horror of Mary of Bethezuba. . . . Maddened by hunger, she seized the infant at her breast and said, "Poor baby, why should I preserve you for war, famine and rebellion? Come, be my food . . . ." With that, she killed her infant son, roasted his body, and devoured half of it, hiding the remainder."[9] The stories that Josephus and the Talmud tell of during this period are absolutely heart-rending.

When the Romans finally breached the walls of Jerusalem, they slaughtered countless thousands of Jews, and hundreds of thousands had already died from starvation. In places, the fires that burned through the city were extinguished by the blood flowing in the homes and streets. The Burnt House and Wohl Archaeological Museum in the Jewish Quarter of the Old City today show signs of the burning that destroyed Jewish homes during that war.

According to Josephus,[10] 97,000 Jewish prisoners were taken when the Romans destroyed Jerusalem. The Romans sent the male survivors who were 17 and older to work as slaves in the mines of Egypt or to be killed in their theatres. They sold into slavery those who were under 17, or took them to be prostitutes in Rome. The Arch of Titus poignantly shows these captured Jews carrying the menorah from the Temple into Rome, where they were later forced to build the Coliseum under inhuman conditions.

When the Romans sent their Jewish captives to Egypt, the slave market was sometimes so glutted that no one bought them. Many of these Jews were then killed by animals or in gladiator matches for the Romans' entertainment.

The Romans exiled the Jews to Babylonia, Egypt, and Rome, and from there the Jews made their way to the ends of the earth.

The documentary hypothesis redactor supposedly lived just after the Babylonian conquest and exile occurred. Why would the Jews think then that they would return to their land and have their own king again, then get exiled again?! They didn't even have their own king until 142 BCE, hundreds of years after the Babylonian exile!

When the Jews came under Christian, then Moslem, rule, they were often forced to worship the wooden cross, and occasionally had to act like Moslems, who worshipped at the rock in Mecca. Over a period of many centuries, the Church forced Jews to convert to their religion or die, lose their livelihood and property, and/or be expelled.

The Torah predicted that the Jews in exile would worship gods that they didn't even know. Islam and Christianity were unknown to the Jews when the Torah was given because these religions began many centuries later.

There were at least seven million Jews before the Roman exile (there were only half a million Chinese at the time.) By the 10th century, there were no more than one-and-a-half million Jews worldwide. There were at least 20 million Jews before World War II, yet there are not more than 12 or 13 million today. Either the Jews should have become as numerous as the Chinese are today, or they should have disappeared entirely into the melting pot of history, as happened to all other conquered and exiled nations.

What mortal author would have predicted this unique historical event of nearly disappearing, then being more numerous than ever before, yet always staying small in number compared to the rest of the world?

Furthermore, the Torah states this:[11]

> *And it will occur, when all of these things have come upon you, the blessing and the curse . . . and you reflect upon them among the nations where the Lord your God has driven you . . . and the Lord your God will restore your fortunes and have mercy on you, and will gather you from all of the nations where the Lord your God scattered you. If your scattered ones are at the ends of the heavens, from there the Lord your God will gather you and from there He will take you. And the Lord your God will bring you to the land which your fathers inherited, and you will inherit it, and He will be better to you and make you more numerous than your ancestors. And the Lord your God will remove the barriers from your heart and from your children's hearts so that you can love the Lord your God with all of your heart and with all of your soul so that you can live.*

How could a human redactor of the Torah have predicted that the Jews would live in exile longer than any other people in history (more than 1,800 years), still retain their religion, and return to their homeland? No civilization in world history has ever done this, except for the Jews.

Mark Twain wrote the following:

> If the statistics are right, the Jews constitute but one percent of the human race. It suggests a nebulous dim puff of star dust lost in the blaze of the Milky Way. Properly the Jew ought hardly be heard of, but he is heard of, has always been heard of.
>
> He is as prominent on the planet as any other people, and his commercial importance is extravagantly out of proportion to the smallness of his bulk. His contributions to the world's list of great names in literature, science, art, music, finance, medicine, and obtuse learning are also way out of proportion to the weakness of his numbers.
>
> He has made a marvelous fight in this world in all the ages, and has done it with his hands tied behind him. He could be vain of himself and be excused for it. The Egyptians, the Babylonians, and the Persians rose, filled the planet with sound and splendor, and faded to dream stuff and passed away.
>
> The Greeks and the Romans followed and made a vast noise and they are gone. Other peoples have sprung up and held their torch high for a time. But it burned out, and they sit in twilight now, or have vanished.
>
> The Jew saw them all. Beat them all, and is now what he always was, exhibiting no decadence, no infirmities of age, no weakening of his parts, no slowing of his energies, no dulling of his alert and aggressive mind.
>
> All things are mortal but the Jew. All other forces pass, but he remains.[12]

The survival of the Jewish people and their unique history as predicted by the Torah are both compelling evidence of its divine authorship.

Notes

1. It is interesting to note that ancient societies were notorious for writing fictitious accounts of their battles with other countries that made their country look good, and for omitting historical recordings that made them look bad. For example, only one account of the Exodus written by Egyptians has been found so far. The Egyptians never wrote that they lost any battles. Rather than admit their resounding defeat after they let the Israelites go, the Egyptians wrote that they were victorious over their former slaves! (Following that is a gap of hundreds of years when they recorded almost nothing more of their history, coinciding with the period that the Torah says their society was destroyed.)

    A stone inscription found in Sancherib's palace also has him bragging about besieging the Jewish king Hezekiah in Judea "like a caged bird." Sancherib omitted mentioning that God miraculously killed Sancherib's 185,000 troops and that Sancherib never conquered Jerusalem or Hezekiah!

    The Torah is one of the very few ancient books that records its people's failings and defeats as well as their victories.

2. Albright, William. *Archaeology and the Religion of Israel*. Baltimore, Johns Hopkins Press, 1942.

3. Subsequent excavations have been done and many archaeologists insist that there were no walled cities in Jericho or the city of Ai from 1400 to 800 BCE, the period within which Joshua would have tried to conquer them. The author asked a renowned maximalist Israeli archaeologist, Avner Goren, if he agreed. He did not. He said that walls were found from the period in question, but most of them had been washed away along with the majority of artifacts from that era. He also said that the city of Ai excavated by archaeologists might not be the city of Ai that was conquered by Joshua. Many authorities believe that today.

4. Archaeologists originally based their ideas about domestication of camels on Assyrian texts that dated to the 11th century BCE. Other evidence that has come to light has proven that the Torah's accounts are plausible. R. Bullet believes that camels were tamed before 2500 BCE, while F. E. Zeuner dates it to 2900-1900 BCE. Abraham lived around 1900-1725 BCE. Two hundred camel bones and teeth were excavated in Umm an-Nar, a city on an island near the coast of Oman, together with objects that dated to 2700 BCE. This provides evidence that dromedaries were domesticated long before Abraham lived. A jar filled with camel dung and fragments of camel hair dating to 2500 BCE was excavated east of Iran. This provides evidence that Bactrian camels were probably domesticated by that time. For more details about the dating of camel domestication, see Stichting Biibel, "Domesticated Camels in the Book of Genesis," *Geschiendenis en Archeologie*, September 24, 2000. Hundreds of bones of camels were recently found in Syria in a human settlement. Archaeologists dated them to 10,000 years ago!

    When the author asked a Bible critic why, despite this evidence, he still didn't believe that camels were domesticated before the 11th century, he responded, "That information doesn't prove anything. Maybe they were only eating the camels, but they weren't domesticated and weren't used for other purposes"

5. Aharoni, Yochanan. *Canaanite Israel During the Period of Occupation.* Today, minimalist archaeologists and Bible critics would disagree with his conclusions.
6. Deuteronomy 28.
7. The Talmud attributes this exile to the Jews' causeless hatred of one another, a problem that still continues today.
8. Josephus, *The Jewish War* VI:271.
9. *Ibid.*, VI:193.
10. *Ibid.*, VI:403.
11. Deuteronomy 30:1-6.
12. *Harper's*, September, 1899.

Why Jews Believe God Gave the Torah

While modern science and objective archaeological findings have largely disproven the documentary hypothesis and "higher Bible criticism," let's see why their ideas are also illogical:

1. If the Torah was put together by several authors and a redactor more than 600 years after Moses wrote it, why should *anyone*, let alone billions of people, believe that it was dictated by God and written by Moses? Imagine a stranger walking up to a Jew and saying, "Here's a book about your ancestors. It was dictated by God and written by His prophet 800 years ago. It contains 613 laws that your people were supposed to have been observing for all those years. Do you want to accept it?"

    The Jew would at least ask, "If this is about my ancestors, how come I, my parents, my grandparents, and their parents never heard of this book before? In fact, how come no one I know has ever heard of this book before? And if I was supposed to have been observing 613 laws for the past eight centuries, why am I only hearing about them now?"

2. The Torah says repeatedly that the Jews must *remember* events in their history. One can only remember events that actually happened. The Torah tells the Jews to *remember*, on a daily basis, that God took them out of Egypt. They must *remember* how God gave the Jews the Torah on Mount Sinai and the events that they experienced at that revelation. They must *remember* what the nation of Amalek did to them, attacking them without provocation. They must *remember* what God did to Miriam for maligning her brother Moses' uniqueness as a prophet. And so on.

3. There is an expression, "If there are two Jews, they have three opinions!" Why should Jews, whom the Torah describes as being hard to convince of God's will in the first place, believe in a book that repeatedly exhorts them to remember mere folktales and superstitions? Why should they believe that Moses wrote the Torah at God's command if he didn't? Why should the Jews believe in a history of their people that never

occurred, especially an account that is probably more negative than that of any other society's or religion's books? Why should they embrace a book written by unknown human authors that criticizes them and requires them to observe a rigorous lifestyle of rituals, ethics, and practices? Trying to convince one Jew to change his or her beliefs is difficult enough! Convincing millions of Jews who were scattered about the entire Babylonian empire to suddenly observe the Torah is as unlikely a scenario as one could imagine.

The Torah says that the Jews were so skeptical and stiff-necked that they weren't willing to follow Moses' directives from God unquestioningly. What kind of bookseller could have convinced them to stake their lives on a book that tells them to remember things they had never known about, heard about, nor experienced?

Nonetheless, although the Torah recounts the Jews' numerous arguments with Moses, there isn't one time they contested the divinity of the Torah. There is no mention anywhere in the Torah that even one Jew refuted the idea that the entire Jewish nation heard God speak to them at Mount Sinai.

Throughout history, millions of Jews were murdered by pagans, Christians, and Moslems for refusing to deny their belief in one God and His Torah. Who could have convinced these people to die for a sloppily written, late-coming hodgepodge of folk tales and irrelevant rituals, as the Torah is portrayed by Bible critics?

4. Who got Jews in disparate communities around the world to believe in a humanly concocted Torah? By the year 500 BCE (according to secular dating), when critics say the Torah was redacted, Jews had already lived in Israel for over 700 years. They had had judges, prophets, kings, a Tabernacle, and a Temple. They had been exiled by the Assyrians and the Babylonians, their Temple had been destroyed, and they had been scattered to the ends of the earth. Yet no matter where Jewish communities were found, they read from and studied

the same Torah. They observed the same holidays and ritual laws, and worshipped the same God with similar services.

In fact, communities of the lost tribes, which were exiled from Israel in the 8ᵗʰ century BCE, had the same Torah and observed the same Torah rituals as Jews who were in the "mainstream" Diaspora further west. If the Torah were only made up in the 5ᵗʰ or 6ᵗʰ century BCE, this would have been impossible. Jews from the western and some of the far-flung eastern communities had no contact with one another until the 19ᵗʰ or 20ᵗʰ centuries.

What redactor, or redactor's publicist, was able to convince Jews in every community around the Diaspora to accept the same book that mysteriously appeared out of nowhere? Even more amazing, who convinced these millions of Jews to live by its detailed rituals that impacted their daily lives?

5. Whatever would have impelled four anonymous authors and a redactor to write a book of idiosyncratic folk stories and bizarre ritual laws? Why would they care if this book's commandments and stories were passed on to future generations? Why would the redactor think that he must convince the entire Jewish people that these stories were true, and that observing these man-made laws was critical to the world's spiritual survival? Moreover, why did a group of people playing such an important role preserve their anonymity?

We could find a plausible motivation had the authors wanted to promote themselves by writing a book that had their names on it. Had God never commanded anyone to observe these laws, it would have made sense for humans to concoct a much simpler, appealing, self-serving, and pleasurable code of living. Most people would much rather subscribe to a book that commands us to eat chocolate every day and watch movies than one that tells us to fast once a year and give tithes from our income to strangers.

6. The Torah is often critical of the Jews. It calls them stiff-necked and portrays their every shortcoming and flaw. Virtually every history book of ancient civilizations exaggerates the people's virtues and accomplishments and omits their failings, except for the Torah. Why should the Jews willingly appropriate a book that portrays them in such a negative light unless there was a divine imperative to do so?

7. While the Torah promises divine blessing for living a Godly way of life, it promises punishment if the Jews don't observe a very exacting list of 613 commandments. These prohibit the fun things that most ancient nations enjoyed—murder, theft, cult prostitution, idol worship, sex with whomever and whenever one wanted, and eating whatever and whenever one wanted. The Torah put many dietary restrictions on the Jews. Sexual abstinence was required for married couples on a regular basis. Male babies had to be circumcised. Jews had to be scrupulously honest in business. They had to give a significant portion of their crops and livestock to the Temple priests and to the poor. Males had to leave their homes three times a year, with their crops untended and their fields unprotected, to make pilgrimages to the Temple. They could not plant nor harvest crops every seventh year, nor work on the weekly Sabbath and yearly holidays, a concept unheard of, and sometimes ridiculed, in the ancient world. They had to rid their homes of all leavened foods once a year and fast for twenty-four hours every Day of Atonement. Men had to wear fringed garments and wind leather straps (called *tefillin*) around their head and arm every day. They had to observe detailed laws of ritual purity and impurity. The list goes on and on. Why would anyone in his right mind do this just because a redactor's public relations agent told him God said that he should?

Early Christianity was only able to successfully take hold with pagans once Paul told them that they should dispense with the ritual laws of the Torah. Even he admitted that the Torah was divinely given. He just believed that the Jews had lost their status as the Chosen People and that they couldn't possibly observe all of the Torah's laws.

8. The documentary hypothesis dates the first author of the Torah to hundreds of years after the Jews received the Torah, and long after they entered the land of Israel under Joshua's leadership. Why would a people to whom God never spoke, and whose revelation they never received, put themselves in the suicidal position of trying to conquer a land that was inhabited by well-entrenched and formidable foes? The Jews had been slaves for 210 years in Egypt, then students in a wilderness for forty years. Whatever would have possessed them to try to conquer strongly fortified cities in the land of Canaan? Jewish doctors, lawyers, accountants, and businessmen would have had the good sense to stay home and make do with the same comfortable and familiar surroundings they had enjoyed for the past four decades! They had no personal incentive to leave where they had been living.

9. After Moses died, the Jews spent fourteen years conquering and settling the land of Israel. By Solomon's era, which is when the documentary hypothesis dates the first piece of the Torah, the Jewish people had been following the laws of the Torah for almost four hundred years. Gentiles, including the Queen of Sheba, came from around the world to see Solomon's Temple, built according to Biblical specifications. These visitors admired the Jews' way of life. Non-Jewish Ethiopians even have an oral tradition about their queen visiting Solomon!

By the time Solomon resigned, Jews had already observed for hundreds of years the detailed laws of ritual purity, Temple sacrifices, and priestly obligations that appear in the Book of Leviticus. They had a system of social justice that encompassed the laws in Deuteronomy that modern critics assert didn't appear for another two centuries.

The dating of the "books" by the Documentary Hypothesis simply doesn't accord with the reality of how the Jews lived. By the time the Torah would have been finalized (by around 500 BCE according to secular dating), the Jews had already been conquered and exiled by both Assyrians and Babylonians. This was a divine punishment for neglecting the laws of the Torah, and had been predicted by the prophets hundreds of years earlier!

If the Torah had only appeared in the fifth century BCE for the first time, it would have been largely irrelevant to the Jews. Their central place of worship had been destroyed and they were not even living in their homeland. If the Jewish Bible hadn't already been part of their lives, they would surely have assimilated into the melting pot of Babylonian society during the century or so that elapsed between their exile and the "appearance" of the redactor's book.

10. The Torah tells the Jews to do certain nearly suicidal things and promises that if they obey God, He will protect them. For example, it was forbidden to plant crops or sell them commercially in Israel every seventh (sabbatical) year. The Torah promises that if the Jews observe the sabbatical years, He will command His blessing on them during the sixth year, and their abundant produce will tide them over into the ninth year! Even the most gullible Jew would not try this a second time if the promise didn't materialize the first time around! What mortal authors would dare make such an outrageous claim? And if they did, who would continue to follow them if the crops ever failed to produce as promised?

Similarly, the Torah requires all Jewish males to go to God's Sanctuary during the holidays of Tabernacles (*Succot*), Passover, and the Feast of Weeks (*Shavuot*). At such times, no one was left to defend the borders of Israel for weeks on end, since traveling to and from Jerusalem could take weeks. We know that the Jews' neighbors were not a friendly lot. These hostile neighbors would not have to be rocket scientists to realize that the land was left unprotected at the same three times every year. Yet the Torah promises that the Jews' neighbors would not desire their land at these times, and in fact, enemy attacks never occurred during these pilgrimages. What mortal authors would dare make this promise?!

11. The Torah lists things that no mortal authors two millennia ago could know, such as which animals are the only ones with just one kosher sign. To be a kosher animal (one that a Jew is permitted to eat), mammals must have two signs: fully split hooves, such as goats or cows have, and they must chew their cud. The Book of Leviticus (11:2-7) lists which animals are kosher and which not, saying that the camel, hyrax and hare chew their cud but do not have split hooves. It also says that the pig has split hooves but does not chew its cud. No other animals have been sighted anywhere in the world, more than 3,000 years after the giving of the Torah, which have only one of these signs.

   What author of the Torah was prescient enough to divine this?

12. The documentary hypothesis is at a loss to explain the Jews' intense loyalty to a book that is a man-made creation full of inaccuracies and nonsense. Josephus was a Jew who lived in Israel during the first century CE. When he was captured by the Romans during their battle against Yodfat, he betrayed the Jews and gave the Romans information that helped them conquer, kill, and enslave his people. Nevertheless, he wrote the following approximately 500 years after modern Bible critics state the "final Torah" appeared:

   > Despite the many [1,400] years that have already passed [since the giving of the Torah], no Jew has been so bold as to either add to our holy books nor take anything away from them, nor make any changes in them. All Jews drink in, with their mother's milk, the belief that these books are of divine origin; the determination to remain faithful to them; and the willingness to die for them if required. It is not new for numerous Jewish captives, time and again, to endure tortures and deaths in all kinds of arenas,

rather than say one word against our laws and the books that contain them.[1]

Conclusion

Jews believe that God revealed His Torah publicly to over 600,000 adult men, plus women and children, at Mount Sinai, and that Moses wrote it at God's command. It was not whispered quietly to one individual who claimed a revelation. It did not start as a belief of a small cult, whose members then proselytized or martyred people until they said they believed in it, too.

The Jewish religion was adopted by an entire nation of at least two-and-a-half to three million people after they experienced a divine revelation over 3,300 years ago. They passed down this Written Law, together with the Oral Law that Moses received at Mount Sinai, in an unbroken chain from generation to generation. No other book in the world besides the Torah, and no other religion except Judaism, can claim these origins. Nor have any other ideas better explained the origins and rituals of the Jews and the Torah.

Some people choose to believe in the Documentary Hypothesis despite the fact that its basic tenets have been disproven logically, scientifically, and archaeologically. A great deal of objective evidence, as well as logic, supports the idea that Moses wrote the Torah at God's bidding over 3,000 years ago. At that time, it was accepted by the Jewish people as being truthful and binding upon them and their descendants forever.

Notes
1. *Against Apion.*

Dr. Aiken's books currently in print:

The Art of Jewish Prayer

To Be a Jewish Woman

Why Me, God? A Jewish Guide to Coping with Suffering

The Hidden Beauty of the Shema

Guide for the Romantically Perplexed

Tuning In

Genesis—The Untold Story

The Baal Teshuva Book (to be published in 2008)

To order her books, book her for speaking engagements
worldwide, or hire her as a tour guide in Israel, please contact her at
lisaaaiken@hotmail.com
(Please note that there are 3 a's in her email address.)